PRAISE

Dr. King said "There comes a time when silence is betrayal, therefore, now is the time for each of us to speak and vote to change the world, especially our Nation. We are all indebted to Erline Belton for her book, challenging each of us to break our silence and speak the truth in our own time and space.

Rev Dr. Otis Moss, Jr.

———————————————

There are women who are wise, who have accumulated knowledge through experience, book learning, and keen observations of the world in which they live. They deserve to be heard and respected.

And then, there are Wise Womyn like Erline Belton. These are spirit people who live among us but also inhabit a plane of existence that many of us cannot see because we are so weighed down by everyday life.

Wise Womyn, among whom I most definitely count Erline Belton, are spiritual guides placed here on earth to show us how to reach beyond the pain of oppression, of the trials and tribulations of work and trying to live an honest life, of the hardships of broken relationships with children, partners, and colleagues, of the pressures of trying to survive in a capitalist culture where acquisition and material consumption are valued over human dignity, and sometimes human life, and of the seeming fleetingness of love and joy—why can't they last forever?

Erline has written a book that encourages us to speak; to lift our voices in unison to those conversations that reaffirm our humanity, that celebrate our peoplehood, that lift us up and inspire us to live, work, and even protest another day, because our voices matter.

This is also a book to guide us on how to use our voices to challenge conversations that may challenge or test us. Erline asks, *"When you are tested to stand up or speak up to confront a mistruth, a mean-spirited or hurtful act or comment or right an injustice, what do you do?*

The answer is easy—keep reading, finish the book, test her strategies, then pick it up again and reread. Pass it on to a good friend who needs inspiration to have courageous conversations.

Like her first book on building a legacy, this book, *Your Voice Matters: Courageous Conversations You Dare to Have*, will become a well-read guide to a new way of seeing and being in the world.

Dr. Irma McLaurin,
Activist, Anthropologist, Award-Winning Author
Past President of Shaw University

Your Voice Matters

Courageous Conversations You Dare To Have

Your Voice Matters

Your Voice Matters
Courageous Conversations You Dare To Have

Your Voice Matters

Courageous Conversations You Dare To Have

Erline Belton

Lyceum Group Book Publishing

Boston MA   **Phoenix, AZ**

Your Voice Matters
Published by:
Lyceum Group Book Publishing
Boston, MA
Email: erlinebelton@gmail.com

Erline Belton, Publisher / Editorial Director
Yvonne Rose/Quality Press. Info, Production Coordinator
Graphic artist: Kristen Belton-Willis

© Copyright 2020 by Erline Belton
Paperback ISBN #: 978-1-0879-2265-2
Ebook ISBN #: 978-1-0879-2266-9
Library of Congress Control Number: 2020921924

DEDICATION

This book is dedicated to my parents, Curtis and Wilene Belton, my grandparents Mary and Josh Gilmore, and to my children, David, Dawn, Nicole, Billy, Kristen, Scotland, Donnie, and Benny. I am a proud part of you.

All of you have a forever sacred loving place in my heart. You have taught me to live my life in the spirit of constant change, honoring your individuality as we continue to grow together through the joys and sorrows of living, while loving each other through it all.

I would not be who I am today without the ways each of you continue to touch my life.

Thank you, my heart is full of love for each of you. ♥

Your Voice Matters

ACKNOWLEDGEMENTS

♥

OUR WORLD Heals
BY TRUTH BEING TOLD

I would like to acknowledge all the people who have touched my life, you know who you are. You are my family, friends, relatives, professional colleagues, and a world that has given me the honor of living in it as a humble servant doing my best to live a joyful life.

I am truly honored and grateful.......to have a voice I can speak up with, and the courage and love that comes from my heart to speak my truth to you ♥

Your Voice Matters

TRUTH JOURNEY
CONTENTS

FOREWORD
INSIGHT AFFIRMATION

Consciously and holistically elevating and empowering gifted and talented leaders to claim their greatness is my life's work. A common denominator that is universal is that we all have voices within us. Voices that either support and stimulate our growth and expansion, OR voices that stifle us and cause us to stagnate – encapsulating us in a fear of speaking out that leads us to remain silent, swallow hard and allow truth to be buried.

What is it that drives us to retreat and allow situations that we know in our hearts are unjust, unethical, and unacceptable when we weigh them against what we say we value – truth and trust?

That is the very question the author, Erline Belton, examines in this illuminating guide about the reclamation of truth through voice. The question above was the impetus for this artful and compelling "call to embrace courage".

Erline clarifies and shares with us herein an enlightening and relevant definition of *courage*. In French, the word for courage is "*cour*" that means heart; it is defined as "inner *most feeling.*" The Latin word for courage is "*cor*" that also means heart. Courage in the context of this book is *to speak one's mind by telling one's heart.* It is about being heroic enough to speak heartfelt truth…no matter what!

This transformative work has been penned during a time of great longing and a need for authentic truth to be unleashed in the world. It is a time where mankind is awakening to the truth that "all lives matter". This profound guide takes that a step further. It awakens us all to the truth that "our voices matter". It is a call to action for you to be heroic enough to explore where there is truth that is being suppressed in darkness and expose it by bringing it into the light using your voice.

If you take nothing else away from this transformational work, please embrace the truth that "Your Voice Matters". Examine and explore the concepts shared within these pages. Dare yourself to be courageous enough to claim your voice and share it with the world.

Erline Belton is the embodiment of what it means to be a Truth-Teller. She is a Voice of wisdom calling forth courage to speak truth authentically and lovingly. My experience of her was first as an executive coaching client when I was longing to reconnect to my own authentic voice that I had allowed to be silenced and buried within me. Erline guided me through deep self-excavation to discover my soulful vocal cords.

Through examining and exploring the truth buried within my heart, much was revealed to me. The process allowed me to re-learn and re-member how to give voice to my truth in alignment with my values – thus renewing and rebirthing my most authentic self. It was the embryotic stages of a profound period of my life that resulted in my own life's work on how to emerge from emotional entrapment. In effect, the work I did to give voice to my truth allowed me to tell my story and give voice to my own truth in my book *The Gifted Trap...E.M.E.R.G.E. From Gifted to Great!*

Doing this work has allowed me to, using the words of Erline herself, ... *"make the spot where I stand more beautiful and better"*!

I owe a profound debt of gratitude to Erline for being so much more than a coach and a mentor – it is an honor to refer to her as a soulful sister friend. We share a bond that has allowed us both to expand and grow into deeper truth-telling.

The fact that you are reading these words is indeed a sign that you are ready to explore new possibilities regarding how to be OF and IN service to others and to yourself. This book is both an invitation and a call-to-action to dive into a deeper exploration of Self.

Whether this book is a catalyst for a private journey with yourself, or a joint journey with one or more others, it is a journey of Truth, Trust and Transformation. I compel you to use it as a guide to go as deep as you are willing and ready to go.

My hope is that it will do what the author intended – **to open your eyes to do the work you might need to do to become the YOU that can look in the mirror and say…** *"My voice matters. I am proud and at peace with ME for speaking truthfully from the depths of my heart"*.

Your Voice Matters … Courageous Conversations You Dare to Have is a book about LOVE, HONOR, TRUST and TRUTH – loving honoring and trusting that in giving voice to truth your voice matters and that will allow you to make a difference in a troubled world. Accept the dare, be courageous and speak your truth!

- Anne Palmer,
Author of The Gifted Trap
E.M.E.R.G.E from Gifted to Great

INTRODUCTION

My intent for writing this book is to take you on a journey that touches a place in you – your heart. If you believe, like I do, that truth is the way forward … this book is for you. If you do not believe truth is the way forward … this book is for you. I believe the world can change and heal when the truth is told from the heart. I want to encourage you to be willing to take a chance. To stand up using your voice to speak up for the truth, that lays on your heart. Allow your courageous self to step into full view. Show the world who you are. Say proudly, this is where I stand. Say I am here to be heard. As you take off and fly, I ask you to remember that your own discovery is only part one of a two-part journey.

Thankfully, there is always another person or other persons to consider to invite into your world of courageous conversation. As you engage them, be understanding and appreciate their difference as a gift to you. This is where speaking what is on your heart, speaking what you feel, and speaking what you think begins. It is a personal challenge that will be both delightful and disappointing at times. This is what your living is all about.

This book speaks to how you can re-script your story by looking inside yourself through self-reflection and curiosity, and by outside yourself with questions that inspire empathy, compassion, and yes, courageous truth. There is a daily Truth mirror practice guide to encourage you to ask, and answer questions. At the end of each story there is the invitation to reflect and write in your journal to tell your story your way.

The intent of this book is to inspire you and to increase your understanding of how and when you speak your truth. Speaking what is on your heart, speaking what you are feeling, and thinking deeply are the pathway to embracing who you are. As you become reacquainted with yourself, my hope is that it causes you to smile. It is not always a comfortable journey; but it is one worth taking.

It is a joy for me to share these insights and real stories of other people lives with you, as they have been told to me. The impact and joy of storytelling is that it can touch us in places you sometimes cannot get to on your own. You will recognize some of the stories as <u>your</u> story. As I listened to the stories, my joys, my pains, my delights, and my disappointments surfaced. All have brought me to a place of wonder, curiosity, and surprise. I am Looking forward to the ongoing adventure of living my life truthfully in the moments as they present themselves, as I hope you will be too.

"Your Voice Matters" comes to you with my heartfelt appreciation of your willingness to take this leap of faith into your journey forward. It will offer you awareness and insights lifting some of the same feelings I have felt to your consciousness and others you did not know were there. I Know and trust that as you take the journey, you can and will make the spot where you stand in our world beautiful, simply because ... **your voice matters!**

Thank you...
Enjoy your journey,
Erline ♥

Your Voice Matters

ONE
COURAGEOUS CONVERSATIONS
YOU DARE TO HAVE

Let it be Known Let it be said...

*The eyes believe themselves: the ears believe others, and the
heart believes the truth. - Ibo proverb*

ETHICS OF TRUTH:
There is no other voice like your own: Your voice Matters ♥

Having courageous conversations you dare to have simply
requires just one important intention from you – to speak what
you feel on your heart, and to say it truthfully to heal, no matter
the consequences.

Your voice has an important place in your world, and there is
no other voice like yours. Speaking truth in a voice you recognize
as your own is where" happy" lives, and that is what you are here

to do -live happy. So, the question becomes, why keep your truth inside where no one can hear it but you?

Over time, I have learned that what I regret most in my life are the things I <u>did not</u> say or do. Joseph Campbell, an author, once said, "The cave you fear to enter holds the treasure you seek."

Is it possible that your voice speaking what is true for you holds your treasure? Speaking your truth is not necessarily an easy path to take. With it comes consequences intended and unintended. It is a journey of choice you take alone. It demands that you ask yourself with heartfelt honesty, *what prevents you from speaking your truth?* The answer to this question opens the door to other issues that might surprise you. Taking time to answer them requires your intention and attention. It will raise your consciousness to a place where you feel and experience personal honor and integrity.

The ethics and practice of courageous truth-telling conversations present itself as a complex social, personal, and human moral dilemma that exposes who you are. It can be heart-wrenching, or it can bring tremendous joy and relief. This practice is not about conformity; it is about transforming yourself to be authentically you. Courageous self- truth builds character and provides you with guidance and a moral compass to guide your way. Speaking truth is uncomfortable at times for most of us, primarily because with it, comes change as you know things to be. Yet, change is what keeps us vibrant and alive; it is a reminder that life does not let you stay in the same place too long.

"Change" moves you from conformity, transforming you into the person you are intended to be. You must be willing to accept change as it adds a voice that unfamiliar to you. The new voice you hear may have questions you have avoided or questions you want answers to. Questions residing in you hold the hidden secrets to answers that explain why you say or do what you do -- as well as, why you chose to remain silent. Questions remind us that the voices inside our head and those on the outside, may be different and must be honored and understood if respectful relationships and connections are to be sustained. Change demands that space must be made to have your powerful voice stand alongside voices that differ from your own. Listening with the sole intent to understand and accept that there are many ways of seeing the same thing is the path forward. We know intuitively and recognize truth when it is spoken from the heart. We must only listen with an open mind and an open heart to receive it and give it back to heal, inspire, offering up our hope and understanding as a gift.

TRUTH ♥

Truth offers itself up as a powerful unifying force that makes the spot where you stand beautiful and welcoming. The caution I offer is to be mindful, knowing truth comes with unexamined bias and prejudice from your personal life experiences. These biases are grounded by your beliefs and values. Left unexamined, they can harden or soften your heart becoming so much a part of your living, that honest self-examination makes it possible or impossible to see or hear another's point of view. Remember, you have your own version of truth stories. They are a part of you and hold your life together or fragment it. Speaking truth to yourself can get foggy. It raises so many questions about the "why" and the "what" – calling on your mind and soul to respond, to choose a path. The most meaningful dialogue that you can have, begins with a truthful conversation from within.

Truth-telling can cause tension and produce uncomfortable silences and natural conflicts that are often misunderstood. It stirs your mind and soul conscientiousness. The real question is, *are you willing to listen, and be challenged by yourself and others? Are you open to accepting new ideas leading to a new awareness and examination of your values and beliefs?* Perhaps it calls for changing the script of the stories you hold that cradle your values and beliefs.

If you chose to take the path of understanding, there is the possibility that truth can unite the dissonance within and outside yourself, as well as, with others. *Should I let it be known, and let it be said?* It is a journey that starts with you and you are alone. As you take the journey, if it is unclear where the path is leading you, go anyway. The journey will introduce you to emotional masks you hide behind that may or may not be evident to you. *Can I hear your truth, will you hear mine?* Understand that as you engage with others, you each come with emotional masks that live inside. The questions for each of you is, *how can we honor each*

8

other, acknowledging we all wear emotional mask to protect ourselves. How can I make space for my truth and your truth to live and breathe together? How can I be sure my truth does not interfere with your soul journey? Or, is it possible that my presence and purpose is to support you as your soul journey unfolds?

As your soul's journey evolves, either as an exploration alone or with others, you will discover places of agreement and disagreement. As they surface, *can you leave room for your perspectives to be different and still change and reshape themselves? Can you allow questions to teach you what you do not know making space for amazing "ahas"?* "OR" which is a powerful word in the English language that offers possibilities. Can you adopt consideration and contemplation to take you to a place of knowing where multiple truths are possible and deserve a conversation where honor and discernment offer up a new opening for truths to emerge?

If you are willing, be still, and take a deep breath; begin to listen to the quiet voice of wisdom from within. You will come to know intuitively that your questions will surface and are there to teach and guide you. It is your sole responsibility and choice to step into your life more fully, speaking with your own voice. Give your voice a chance. Now is the time to say, "See me. I am here. I see you. Can you see me? I have something to say. I am willing to listen and learn." Now is the moment to Claim the Magnificent person you are meant to be.

TRUTH STORY:
Consider Another way of seeing

An artist friend of mine once gave me a valuable life lesson that revealed an alternative way of discerning truth. I hold her insights as an intrinsic treasure to me. We had been talking about truth-telling and the courage it takes to speak truthfully on things that matter to us. We both agreed that truth-telling is one of life's most difficult challenges that just keeps popping up - testing us, again and again. Being the incredibly gifted artist, she is, her artist's eyes influence her way of looking at the world we live in.

We were standing at the seashore engaged in sorting it all out. Suddenly, she pointed to the clouds in the sky and asked me, "how many shades of grey and white do you see?" I had never thought of clouds as having shade gradations, they were just grey or white to me. I looked up, and to my surprise, I saw many shades of grey and white. How could it be that I had never noticed this before? The clouds had always been there, the multiple shades of grey and white lived there too. And, at that moment, they were displaying themselves above us in full view, on a beautiful canvas sky. We watched as the wind with its playful spirit quietly and continually reshaped the clouds, causing the light of the Sun to come through. A magnificent color palette of grays and whites danced gracefully together and changed their color and shapes in each moment. As our eyes took in the beauty of their movement and changing transformation, they were still clouds displaying their calming magnificence. In retrospect, I wonder what she saw.

There is no doubt in my mind that we saw the clouds differently, and that was the silent beauty in the moment we shared.

Then, she asked me the same question again as we stood looking at the waves coming on to the shore. "How many shades of grey and sea green do you see in the sea?" I was so touched by the simplicity of seeing in this new way, a smile of delight came to my face. How could I have lived this long at the seashore, never seeing what was right in front of my face? It occurred to me that her artist's eyes allowed her to see in ways that were not in my consciousness, until she asked me a simple question. What did I see?

I had to be willing to listen to her and to open my eyes to see differently. Sometimes a simple question can totally change our consciousness and reshape the way we see, listen, and experience our lives, circumstances, conversations, and relationships with other people.

It strikes me now that truth is very much like clouds hiding the light of the sun, being shaped by the wind, and colored by the mystical beauty of the sun's hidden glorious rays. *Your truth very often resides in an inner space inside you that cannot be seen by others who are looking at and hearing the same thing, yet, hearing and seeing it differently.*

Your truth can be hidden behind the clouds of thoughts in your private world, waiting for the opportunity to be revealed. Patiently waiting for the right question to get asked to move you to your spoken truth. Albert Einstein once said, "Questions are the things that teach us." Questions can become transformative connectors when they come from the heart and happen naturally with a playful spirit that allows us to see with our eyes, our mind, and listen with our hearts wide open.

Speaking truth's only purpose is to heal the one who is speaking, as well as the one who is listening. Truth, like the many hues of grey and white in the clouds as seen with the human eye, has many colors. Choosing to have courageous conversations is in some ways like clouds. There is a reshaping that takes place from dark to light, once spoken. You may be in a space where speaking the truth feels like dark clouds. It is when you remember dark clouds can be transformative. Clouds can separate and reshape themselves in new revolutionary ways. Speaking truth is like the clouds, your voice reshapes what truth is for you as you speak. If you are willing to allow the magic of sunlight in, new insightful truths can be revealed to you.

TRUTH STORY:
Leave An opening for truth-Awareness,
what are you doing? Why?

A friend shared a personal story with me about a relationship where money concerns had caused continual tension in the relationship. It was the constant elephant in the room any time money was the topic between her and her partner. During one of her many conversations discussing money issues, her partner spoke his truth as he knew it, "it's all about the money, isn't it?" The intention behind asking the question was to put her on the defensive, as it always had in the past. She realized at that moment that she had a decision to make. Would she quiet her voice to avoid the tension and keep a false calmness between them? Her experience told her it was easier to keep the peace by suppressing what she really felt, minimizing unpleasant anxiety. Instead of defaulting to her usual behavior of silencing herself, she chose at that moment to speak her truth story. "Yes, it is," she said. To her surprise, an amazing thing happened. The world did not come to an end, and they had a tough, but truthful, conversation that led to a radical change in his behavior. Ultimately, his focus moved towards committing to taking steps to secure the financial security they both needed. Her moment of speaking courageously what was true for her changed their relationship, making it stronger, as opposed to keeping a fragile dishonest peace hidden behind dark clouds of unspoken words.

This reminds me of my oldest son, who is a closet comedian and offers humor every chance he gets. He has a saying that I find amusing and insightful in its humor. It may be helpful to share it here. He can be heard saying, when things get tense, *"Let it be known. Let it be said."* There is great wisdom that resides in that simple phrase, and I suspect it is where freedom to tell our authentic story lives for all of us.

REFLECTION 1.
BE STILL…ASK…LISTEN…BE STILL

Reflection and Curiosity: What are inner truths you must say out loud, that have not been spoken? ♥

1. What dark clouds of truth reside in you that need to be spoken?
2. What is in it for you to keep your truth hidden?
3. What is in it for you to let the truth be said and let the truth be known?
4. What is your greatest fear of speaking your truth?
5. What needs to happen for you to feel safe to speak your true story?

REFLECTION 2.
JOURNALING …BE STILL…ASK …LISTEN…. WRITE….BE STILL

Can you open your heart to –Speak your mind?

What both fascinates and saddens me is that courageous conversations rarely happen. They reside in dark clouds of fear. If you would only dare to silence your voice and take time to listen, to part clouds, that may be hovering inside. This can provide the opening for a way forward in your relationships or circumstances that can be freeing.

Some of those spaces will feel awkward and uncomfortable at first. They may even cause you temporary pain. Some, like my friend's conversation with her partner, can open a space allowing a welcomed behavioral shift. It is only possible when you are willing to take that 1st step and risk speaking out loud about what is hiding behind your emotional masks, your own dark clouds. Like the clouds reshaping themselves, you provide the space and possibility for light rays to shine on you and the lives you are destined to touch.

What does the "Ethics of Truth" mean? How can I understand and apply the truth?

To understand the challenges faced in having Truth as the moderator for a courageous conversation, it is useful to clarify the definition of *courage*. In French, the word for courage is *"cour,"* which means heart; *it is defined as "innermost feeling." The Latin word for courage is "cor", which also means heart – to speak one's mind by telling one's heart.* Over time the meaning has changed to mean heroic.

The Cambridge Dictionary defines conversation as a talk between two or more people in which thoughts, feelings, and ideas are expressed, questions are asked and answered. In the old French Word Dictionary, the definition is *"a manner of conducting oneself in the world."*

These definitions of courage and conversation are helpful joining two words together to form a powerful concept, The Ethics of Truth.

Consider this as a definition for ***Courageous Conversations;*** *how you conduct yourself as you speak, telling what is in your heart; engaging with another person or persons; sharing your thoughts, inner feelings, ideas; opening the door for questions to be asked, answered, listened to and acted on as you explore new ways of speaking and being fully present for one another.*

It begins with **you.** It Starts with the courage to speak your truth to heal, no matter the consequences. How you engage with others matters. It makes space for questions to be asked, answers to be shared, and really listened to, as evidenced only by a change in behavior. As the behaviors change it is a good time to acknowledge and understand that values and beliefs are shifting to a new place to support the behavior change.

There is likely agreement for most, at least intellectually that you want to live, work, and have relationships where speaking what is on your mind and in your heart, is acceptable. The intellectual part is natural, it is the emotional investment and courage you must embrace to have conversations that reveal your innermost feelings. This is the place where tummy churning stress begins its life. As we rehearse trying to get just the right words and say it the right way. We experience internal noise and conflict. However, when you do gather the courage to talk about your innermost feelings, you will experience peace as you know and feel yourself speaking from a place of loving power.

If you are truthful with yourself, you live and breathe each moment with an expectation of honesty in your relationships and in your conversations with others. This is a comforting quality to live by. It is when situations evoke controversy that you have reason to pause and be thoughtful. It takes personal courage today to state your views on some of the pressing social issues of our times. Sensitive issues require serious deliberation and engagement.

Never in the history of our country have the issues been more polarizing. Compromise is a dirty word, seemingly out of reach. Families, friends, colleagues, and political parties and social policies cannot be discussed for fear of political incorrectness offending someone. Resolution and finding common ground seem almost impossible. Your innermost feelings are suppressed and rarely shared. The conversations that really matter to you go unspoken.

We are in a crisis where we shut down our personal views on topics where our political ideology, injustice, discrimination, sexual orientation, religious beliefs, race relations, situations at work are different from others. Peaceful protests are defined as "mobs" with the disruptions by a few invoking fears, to keep us from reaching for each other, pushing us further apart. Complex family secrets, as well as, these things, all represent dark clouds with no seeming possibility of light rays shining through. Any one of these topics is avoided deliberately to keep the peace. Yet they require courageous conversations if we are ever going to reach and embrace one another as one. We must reach for and embrace each other to save ourselves. We can do this.

It may seems the easier choice is to keep silent allowing a fragile peace to exist. If you take the time to examine yourself truthfully, you will find your tendency is to shy away from making waves because it may cause tension, making people uncomfortable, forcing you to choose what side you are on. Why is it not ok in our world today, to decide what side you are on and not be judged or rejected? Do you choose to stand with or back down? Only you can make the choice.

TRUTH STORY:
Children's Courage unfiltered Truth

Children in their innocence can teach us a lot in this space about speaking our truth when standing alone. My grandson and I were talking about truth-telling, and he told me a story that illustrates this beautifully. His son was only 4 years of age and already had a commanding presence with a personality that defined him as a compassionate and outspoken young boy. He is precocious, delightfully joyful, and observes and takes in everything he sees and hears. He is often the source of amusement for those in his presence. You never know what will come out of his mouth.

At a family gathering, a friend came in, seeing Jaxson; he smiled happily to see him. He asked for a high 5, in greeting. My great-grandson looked at him, crossed his arms in defiance, and said no. Mind you, this was a long-time family friend who he knew and trusted. The friend was taken aback. When the friend asked him, "why not," he said simply, "because I don't like you." The friend was silent, as was everyone else within range. There was a moment of discomfort, and everyone moved on. As adults, there would have been a vastly different conversation probably one that was less than direct. It would have been riddled with politically correct explanations to ease the tension.

His father was stunned, and his first instinct was to say that is not nice; thankfully he held himself back. As my grandson was trying to understand what caused this response in his son, he remembered a previous backyard barbeque where a slight altercation occurred between the friend and his wife. Voices were raised and there was silent tension in the air. My great-grandson witnessed this and was obviously affected by it. It changed his truth story about the family friend. The behavior towards his wife was seemly unimportant and forgotten by others; but, for the little guy, it was not. It changed his relationship and feelings for the family friend, and when given a chance, Jaxson expressed truthfully how he felt about him. He spoke what was true for him, standing alone, not looking for allies.

How many of us would have had the courage of this 4-year-old? For most of us, we would hold onto the story, keeping it hidden because it evoked uncomfortable feelings and emotions. My grandson told me later that while he was shocked when his son spoke his truth, he was secretly proud of his son for speaking up and admitted to me he had to suppress his laughter when it happened.

TRUTH STORY:
Children and straight talk, just imagine raw truth

Young children are often our truth-bearers. I remember when my son was only 3, we were in an elevator and someone passed gas. My son said out loud, "It stinks. Someone farted." It was all I could do to hold back the laughter. I made it worse by saying, "That's not nice." He came right back with, "Well, it sure stinks." I felt like a real jerk at that moment. He was right. It did stink.

A friend of mine told me a story about her niece, who was studying French. My friend thought she spoke French very well and offered to help her niece with her homework. After translating something from English to French, her 8-year-old niece said, "auntie, you really should not speak French, "you are not particularly good at it." She was hurt by her niece's words. Out of the mouth of babes, truth.

It would be fantastic if you could stand in this kind of reality. To stand with a pure, authentic, and loving voice, not considering the consequences. A voice that comes from your heart, no judgment or hurt intended.

So, the questions you must ask yourself are: *How do I begin to understand this? How do I find my own unique voice?* What excellent questions to ask yourself?

It all starts with questions. It is an entirely internal dialogue that gives you truthful answers, whether you like them or not. Once you ask yourself the questions, the actions you take based on what you learn is the journey.

REFLECTION 1.
BE STILL...ASK...LISTEN....BE STILL

Reflection and Curiosity: How can you bring your childlike innocence forward to speak truth? ♥

1. Is there anything you are not giving voice to that matters or impacts you?

2. What keeps you from choosing to speak your truthful innermost feelings?

3. What do you imagine will happen if you speak what is true for you?

4. What would it feel like to stand alone in your truth and speak it out loud?

5. Are you willing to make space to be quiet and listen to your internal voice?

6. What are the questions you must ask and answer to get clear?

7. What one action are you willing to take guided by your internal voice?

REFLECTION 2.
JOURNALING...BE STILL.... LISTEN...WRITE....BE STILL...READ

TWO

IT BEGINS WITH YOU...
YOUR VOICE MATTERS

If you are always trying to be normal, you will never know how amazing you can be -Maya Angelou

Courage to acknowledge, Unfinished business is your business.

How often have you held back words that you knew needed to be spoken? What conversations have you not had because you felt you would not be heard or listened to, because your words would make people uncomfortable? How often have you been silent to the outside world, while within, your internal dialogue continually rages, repeating itself, not letting you rest?

It is in your heart; it permeates your mind and soul. Those conversations not had, stay present with you as a constant reminder that **you do** have unfinished business. Your conscious and unconscious mind seem at odds with one another, asking you to face choices you would rather not make. Remember that unfinished business is your business.

Ask yourself, *what is my unfinished business? Why can't I speak on issues that matter to me? How do I say what I am feeling to the person who is central to my discomfort?* Perhaps you learned early what could not be talked about in your family; sometimes, you were even punished. You learned to just shut up, as members of your family reprimanded you, causing confusion within when the obvious truth was in plain sight. Some things were just not spoken, even when everyone present was a witness to the truth. There seemed to be an unspoken rule that held your family to a code of silence that you did not understand. There were questions jumbled in your young mind. *Will I get in trouble? Should I say it? Will I mess it up? Will I be excluded or rejected from the family?*

Those lessons you learned so very long ago created your true-life story that you carried into adulthood. Just shut up and go along with it. Just stay quiet, do not make a fuss or you will be punished. You learned early if you remained silent, everything would be OK. You learned early how to live in false, fragile relationships where you silenced your voice, and It has had a lasting effect. Moving forward, it is essential for you to acknowledge what you learned and to ask yourself the question, "Is silencing my voice serving me well on my life journey right now?" If it is, hold on to it. However, if it is not, let the habit of silencing your voice go. Finish your unfinished business by speaking your truth. Contrary to what you have been taught to believe …Your voice matters.

TRUTH STORY:
When Silence is a personal betrayal of who you are.

Allow me to share another story that happened to me and a friend where fear and embarrassment got in the way of a person being who they knew themselves to be.

A friend and I were standing at an ice cream stand. It was a very disorganized waiting line; people were just standing all over the place. Unsure of who was in line and who wasn't, my friend and I walked up to two senior ladies in front of us. I asked if they were in line or waiting for their order. One of the ladies responded in an angry voice, "Don't you see me standing here?" In retrospect, I find myself wondering whether race was a factor in this scenario. My friend and I are African Americans, and they were Caucasians. I was taken aback at her hostility and replied, "I was only trying to be polite. I did not want to get in front of you." My immediate reaction was to be angry. Here I was trying to be respectful, and she responded to me with hostility that was not warranted from where I stood. Of course, I did not know what her life was like that day. My friend and I felt like slapping her. Then I remembered, "The Four Agreements" by Don Miguel Ruiz. One of which says, "don't take things personally." It was hard to quiet my emotions, but I let my unhealthy feelings go.

Unexpectedly, the most heartwarming thing happened next. The woman who was so abrasive left. Her friend was standing in front of me, waiting for her ice cream. She turned to me and asked, "Are you the woman my friend was so rude to?" I said,

"Yes." She said sheepishly, "I want to apologize for my friend. I just could not bring myself to say anything then. I didn't know how my friend would take it."

It must have taken a great deal of personal courage for her to speak up, not knowing how I would respond. I said, "I appreciate your apology." Thankfully, I had calmed down enough to leave room for accepting her apology.

Why do you remain silent in situations where you risk rejections or stand-alone in your thinking when you see an injustice being done? What is it that holds you back when you know that what is happening is just not right? In this instance, the woman who apologized to me could not look me straight in my eyes. She was ashamed. I can only assume that she did not want to embarrass her friend, or perhaps lose her friendship over this unpleasant experience.

In this instance, she preserved her friendship and had the chance to apologize for her friend in private, redeeming herself from the self-inflicted internal anguish brought on by remaining silent. She knew what was happening was disagreeable to her, yet she made a choice to remain silent. I am left wondering how she felt about herself later because of her silence. In effect, she was complicit in condoning her friend's behavior by remaining silent while she was still present. I can only hope the woman who apologized to me could forgive herself. In saying I appreciated her apology; I forgave her silence. I know I felt better, and I moved on.

Dr. Martin Luther King once said,

*"Our lives begin to end the day we become
silent about things that matter."*

TRUTH STORY:
Truthful Intimacy in Relationships

Truthful relationships all have intimacy involved, yet many of us do not see it this way. Intimacy is about more than having a satisfying sexual relationship. True intimacy is a way of being with one another in friendship or in a relationship with a partner. Expression of true intimacy often does not require words. Imagine that. It can be a smile that touches your heart when you need it most. It can be a tender touch, cuddling, hugs when least expected, or just kinds words. Its being caring and loving to one another.

On the other hand, when words are required, they must be an expression that speaks truth of your inner most feelings. I am reminded of a children song I used to play on the guitar in the Day care center where I worked as Director. The children loved it because it allowed them to express themselves outwardly and openly with enthusiasm. It goes like this: When your happy and you know it clap your hands when your sad and you know it stomp your feet, if your happy and you know, if your sad and you know it, then you really ought to show it. There is so much wisdom in this children song, to simply show and say what you feel. Intimacy in relationships goes sour when you do not say or show what you feel.

Stories of sexual intimacy almost always take on a more secretive quality. The truth of your sexual experience most often is not spoken between couples for fear of losing a relationship. Thoughts of expressing what is real produces denial, anxiety, and extremes in emotional reactions – sometimes surprise, discomfort and or relief can happen. It is the anticipation of what can happen if you own up to intimate untruth where your pretended sexual satisfaction, to feed comfort, and diminish discomfort for yourself and your partner. Your lack of expression silenced your voice.

When you think about the impact of truthful words not spoken between you and your partner by not speaking your happy or your sad and you know it. It can feel heavy and sad causing you unhappiness.

Many of the stories I heard noted painful emotions wrapped up in pretense of outward emotional expression and body movements suggesting pleasure. In truth all you really wanted was for the sexual act to be over with. You believed you convinced your partner it was great. The real deal is many times your partner knows it is not, and it was not. Neither of you has the courage to speak on it because it is not worth the risk of hurting his or her feelings. In fact, it is a charade you both collude in to save face for you and your sexual partner in the intimate space you share together.

Pretending creates awkward moments in intimate sextual relationships in the bedroom. Truth liberates loving. How on earth is it going to get better, or does it just get bitter. This silence wounds and hurts both partners. Hidden by your emotional mask, it causes a silent discomfort and damages and sabotages the relationships most of you want to keep in the long run. Relief comes when it is spoken about truthfully and openly. The outcome may or may not be what you want, but it will brings you another way of being in truth together.

It is a universal truth; you experience unimaginable gratification when you give voice to what is true for you. Once you open the door to speak what is in your heart, you have space to hear what is true for someone else. Give it a try with your friends and your partner.The truth in the end always has a way of coming out, and we know intuitively when the truth is spoken. This, in turn, leaves room for forgiveness and healing.

REFLECTION 1.
......BE STILL...ASK ....LISTEN...BE STILL

Reflection and Curiosity: How do I see myself in intimate relationships with others ♥

1. Are there situations where you have remained silent, and wish you had not?

2. How did you feel and what did you give up by not speaking up?

3. What do you wish you had said or done differently?

4. Are there conversations you need to have to retire unfinished business in relationships where you have remained silent?

5. How can you prepare yourself to listen, ask questions, have questions asked of you, as you open your heart and mind to what you have avoided?

6. Are you willing to be truthful and forgiving in intimate relationships that matter to you?

7. If yes, Why? If no, Why not? What will you do to make it better?

REFLECTION 2.
JOURNALING...BE STILL...LISTEN...WRITE...BE STILL, READ

THREE
WHAT IS AT STAKE?
A CHANCE TO RESCRIPT YOUR STORY

The ultimate measure of a man is not where he stands in moments of comfort, but where he stands in times of challenge and controversy. - Dr. Martin Luther King, JR

What is at stake here is your opportunity to discover a vibrant new life force opening inside you, just waiting to debut on your stage. You can rewrite the script and give voice to what you believe. It is an opportunity to expand, be vulnerable and expose proudly who you are. It takes a lot of courage and requires taking risks to speak up, reach out, stretch, and go to places you have not gone to before. It takes courage to stop or move forward. Engaging yourself and others, as you cultivate your unique imprint that defines your living legacy. What is at stake here is your choice to do all you can do using your voice to stand in your own words, to live your best life.

When you are tested to stand up or speak up to confront a mistruth, a mean-spirited or hurtful act or comment or right an injustice, what do you do? What have you done in your past? What do you want to do going forward? Honorable Congressman, John Lewis, urges us to cause Good Trouble, Necessary Trouble. To not stop but to continue to push forward for the changes we seek.

This could be your moment, your opportunity to shine and re-define who you are for yourself and others. This is where the word courage becomes actionable and can take on real meaning. Your conscience may be of two minds – one urging you to voice your opinion, "Yes, you need to speak up. Speaking up is the right thing to do;" and the other might be reprimanding you, "Do not be crazy, just keep your mouth shut. You could be punished." At this moment, the most limiting thought you can have is that you have no choice in voicing what matters to you. When, in fact, you do. Choice by choice, moment to moment, your voice matters.

Consider this, what is also at stake is your integrity and the freeing of your spirit and soul. How you give voice to the truth as you understand it is a personal revolutionary act. The truth of your experiences of life is your own story. It defines you and how you show up in each moment. It is continuously up for contemplation and a re-write because it represents your unique imprint. Your imprint defines you and your legacy, and it will change as you learn and grow. It speaks constantly to who you are, what you believe, and what you stand for as a person as you live your life.

You are, thankfully, different. You see and experience your world differently than any other human being. You are the gift to conversations and situations you encounter. No matter how risky it might seem, your value as a person is what your voice represents.

Courageous conversations, particularly in times of stress and uncertainty, must be guided by your beliefs and values. They provide the rich text for your script as you speak with honorable heartfelt intentions. Your beliefs and values are the backdrops that honor all of who you are, and all of whom the other person is.

Can you accept that there are infinite possibilities beyond your personal point of view? As you engage with one another, can you trust that some greater plans, thoughts, or ideas may be revealed to you? It is in these moments where the best thing you can do is to listen intently, with your ears and hearts open; realizing that your questions are teachers and are just as important as the answers you receive.

Speaking truth of what is in your heart can open the door to encourage others to do the same. It can also shut them down. Who knows what the possible outcome will be? What you do in each moment sets in motion an opportunity for a new voice, healing, or idea to emerge. It offers an opportunity for alternative pathways to be revealed, generating new thoughts, solid relationships, vibrant communities, and gives our world a chance to grow and heal.

Will it be you who is the one to stand up, to bring courageous conversations to the surface?

Is it you who will take the risk and say, "This is just not so?" Will you be the one to say, "There is another version of this story that must be told?" Is it you who will ask the questions that people are afraid to ask, the ones that are considered the unspeakable ones? If not, you...then who?

I am not suggesting that breaking fragile silence is comfortable. Quieting yourself to hear the voice inside you that is urging you to speak thoughtfully requires that you be willing to take the risk to be vulnerable – that you learn to trust your intuition and act on it. It is a time when maturity is what is needed to move conversations forward. Accept that it may not go the way you would like. Yes, there is always the possibility of disappointment. There is also the possibility of opening a space for the right relationships to be strengthened or rebuilt, based on openness and trust.

Collusion with silence can become so much a part of our truth story that it inhibits our freedom as individuals. The impact of voices repeatedly going unheard is all too common today in our society seeping over into our families, relationships, organizations and our world. When everything is polarized, and compromise is not seen as an alternative, we all lose.

It is common today to assume, that no one cares enough or is willing to acknowledge or talk about things that matter deeply to them. The things that lay on your hearts stay dormant. The silence that prevails as a result is suffocating. It calls for a voice; any voice, one voice that can make a difference by breaking the silence. It is not until someone is courageous enough to stand up, to speak their truth out loud publicly that a remarkable exhale can happen.

This longed-for breath becomes the salve to free your spirit and begins to heal the hurt and wounds caused by silence. Your voice could be that game changer that leads towards healing and openness. If it is not your voice, but someone else's, do not leave that voice out there to stand alone; it gets lonely standing by yourself. If it is not your voice, dare to add your voice to one that is willing to stand for what is right and just. To quote a man of greatness and humanity, Dr. Martin Luther King, Jr., in his brilliance, said, *"There comes a time when silence is betrayal."*

Silence is where "scary" lives. It calls out desperately for courage. It takes courage to expose yourself. My wish is that it is you, who will unleash your precious choice to step into a place where you experience the freedom of speech. A place where your presence is felt in a gentle, powerful way, as the chosen one to speak of your truth. I offer you an old Indian saying in support of your courage, *"My heart laughs with joy to be in your presence. Thank you*

Are you scared? It is ok: take a risk

Acknowledging risks and fears and taking that first terrifying step to voice truth that you have dreaded speaking for so long will bring you incredible liberation. When you show up as yourself and say, "This is what I believe! This is who I am! This is where I stand on this issue." It will liberate you. It is plain scary to speak up when you believe you must stand alone. What if your voice will not be heard or misunderstood?

For most of us, we have been play-acting for so long that we create enormous self-doubt in ourselves, confusing what is real and what is imagined. We convince ourselves that it is easier to just go along with the program. We compromise to belong and pretend we are someone we are not. This choice provides us with a measure of false security. You comfort yourself with false beliefs that safety is woven into the dark clouds of silence—that concealment and just going along with the program, will secure our place. Of course, the irony is that when concealment occurs, it is no cover-up at all because everyone knows what needs to be said, yet, no one has had the courage to say it.

Accepting and understanding that fear lives inside you and me is real stuff. Something or someone created our fears of feeling unsafe, and we internalized them as our own. When you feel unsafe, there is little chance that you will take the risk to face your fears. Wounds from silencing your voice are fueled by fear and go underground, buried deeper as time goes on. Your fears will remain unspoken until you acknowledge them and have real evidence that it is safe to voice them.

The behaviors of leaders and others in relationships, families, and organizations must demonstrate that you will be safe and will not be blamed or judged if you do speak the truth. Of course, there is the most powerful fear to be faced. That fear is that, no matter what the consequence, you will have the courage to speak. What is also at stake here is, if left unchecked, fear will continue to hold you hostage, creating tension and stress in your body. It takes up residence as a constant companion. It forces you to ask, how do I need to show up differently? It demands personal examination and clarity that speaks to which side you are on – right or wrong. Living with the uncomfortable feeling that you might not know which side you are on can make your heart and head hurt. Remember, speaking courageously calls for you to be fully who you are.

Fear of what could happen prevails and covers us like ominous threatening clouds smothering us in silence. We know that words have power. What if we say the wrong thing? Or, what if we say the right thing that sets us all free?

It is not what you want to say that is frightening, but what could happen to you after you have said it. There are examples in every aspect of our lives, some perceived and some real where it did not work out well. There are many examples of casualties where people who have spoken up to voice their truth have been fired, rejected by family and friends, isolated, retaliated against, or come under false attack creating painful self-doubt and public ridicule. These actions leave us fearful with emotional scars that do not get talked about. These scars are real living things causing personal discomfort, emotional dread, humiliation – all of which are stored in our memory banks. It is essential to understand that memories represent our reality. This reality is our script that keeps us locked up colluding with untruths and cover-ups, keeping our voice silent with words unspoken and unfinished business.

Intuitively we know there is personal and emotional risk involved here. This kind of exposure almost certainly invites vulnerability and the possibility of being judged fairly or unfairly by the others. So, What!!!!! Taking risks offers the opportunity to experience defining moments of greatness. It provides a chance to discover a new voice you may not be familiar with that resides inside your head and heart, just waiting for the authentic you to show up. It takes courage to stop or to move forward.

If you wish to remain silent when your voice is urging you to speak, you will feel personal disappointment and emotional churn in the pit of your stomach. You will begin to question what you think and feel, rethinking to yourself, creating self-doubt. "Maybe I have it all wrong," is the story you tell yourself. Convincing yourself that perhaps the timing is just not right. You find yourself questioning the validity of your experience and your feelings. To get temporary relief, you delude yourself into thinking, "If I wait a while, it will get better. Or, "Now is not the right time". Or, I'll do it tomorrow." You remain silent, hoping for the best.

Rarely does waiting make it any better. By making a choice to wait, you live with the turmoil inside your head and heart, where your voice engages in internal dialogue, creating a nagging story that competes with your external world of the living. While on hold, you find yourself rehearsing over and over in your mind, what you will say, and how you will say it. This recurring conversation goes on endlessly. It just will not go away. It hurts your heart, dims your spirit, and creates fear about what might happen to you if you have the conversation. It is only when you confront your fears and are honest about your feelings; that you will find your authentic voice.

We all live hoping to get to our authentic self. *Remember, unspoken words have no value to you or anyone else. Please speak up, we need to hear your voice.*

The question that deserves your compassionate attention is, *why do you remain silent?* Why are you holding yourself back from what you know you need to say? Whether your fear is real or imagined, the result is the same. You are being held hostage to your fears.

Are you concerned with the uncertainty of how the person will react to what you must say? It is OK to feel scared, just do not run away. When, where, and how you give your voice permission to speak the truth is a choice, a decision only you can make. It is truly a liberating and powerful moment when you choose to speak from your heart with your voice.

The secret to inner peace and quieting the internal story that lends itself to tension and stress is giving yourself permission to speak. Words are powerful, they are the voice of your heart; they create the bridge you walk across that will take you forward on your life path. The personal challenge you face is, *do you want to be what people need you to be?* Or, *do you want to be your authentic self?* In making a choice to be yourself, you may find that you stand alone. Can you stand alone in your truth, remaining true to yourself, even if it means no one stands with you?

Having courageous conversations, you have been afraid to have up to now offers you a chance to:

1. Acknowledge your fears and take the risk to move through them.
2. Discover the amazing you beyond what others expect,
3. Give voice to your personal imprint that defines your legacy.
4. Offer you the opportunity to complete unfinished business.

It is your opportunity to shift from ordinary to incredible. Go for it!!!

REFLECTION 1.
BE STILL...ASK...LISTEN....BE STILL

Reflection and Curiosity: Do you Understand why You silence your VOICE? ♥

1. What is at stake for you when you silence your voice?

2. What will it take for you to be willing to risk stepping out first?

3. Are you willing to move through your "scary" and stand with someone who stands alone?

4. Imagine opening a space for truth, by someone different than you. What does that feel like?

5. Can you remember a time where you stereotyped and moved to judgment and took an uninformed stance?

6. What was your missed opportunity by doing so?

7. Is there a new script you wish to write for yourself?

REFLECTION 2.
JOURNALING...BE STILL.... LISTEN...WRITE....BE STILL, READ

FOUR
IDENTIFY INHIBITORS:
THE WHATS AND WHYS THAT HOLD YOU BACK?

Don't compromise yourself; you're all you've got
- Janis Joplin

To answer the pivotal question, "What stops you from moving forward?", you must first understand what the inhibitors are for you. They are "The What and Why's," that hold you back?

What stops you? There is never one single factor: several can be living in us because it involves human feelings, emotions, and beliefs that thrive and become a part of who we are as we experience life's ups and downs. Inhibitors gain their strength or dissolve, depending on our personal courage to show what we stand for. It is wrapped up in your personal confidence to examine and acknowledge your fears to make necessary changes. Most of us do not want to be hurt, nor do we want to hurt others. This very real concern creates a fear of rejection and often stops us in our tracks.

Other inhibitors combined with the fear of being hurt or rejected hold us hostage to speaking truth from our hearts. Each of us has a unique perspective that comes from our life experiences. Life has so much to show us from what we know. That is the beauty in our place here on earth; **it is our differences that make the difference.**

Our challenge and opportunity are to open our minds and hearts to honor those differences and understanding; others just might see it differently than we do. Emotional inhibitors, familiar to us all, prevent your authentic voice from showing up to speak the truth. The question is, *how do you want to show up in a different way?* The answer requires that you let go of the current version of who you are and consider becoming the person you want to be.

Remember, Inhibitors are feelings, emotions, past experiences, and just the living of your day to day life. They come with joys and disappointments that have a grip on your soul, going unacknowledged or misunderstood. It is like a human vice that will not let go no matter how hard you try to loosen its grip. They stop movement in your life. It is like being on hold indefinitely until you are ready to push the button to release your "on-hold" status.

The way forward is to become aware of what the inhibitors are, examine them truthfully through self-reflection and have an honest dialogue with yourself, that allows you to commit to the discipline to move on. It takes personal courage to stop or move forward. Once you acknowledge and understand inhibitors, you can relieve Your inner critic as the dominant voice inside, saying words that speak of self-persecution and judgment. This takes consistent discipline and personal risks that have the promise of inspiring changes in you. It is a reminder that disciplined actions offer a solid foundation for your personal freedom to thrive on.

While there are many more inhibitors than I identify here, in my informal research, there are the seven inhibitors that were mentioned most often as the barriers to speaking truth.

1. Tendency to avoid or confront, fearing conflict
2. Self-justification, the need to be right
3. Fear of the consequences, standing in your truth alone
4. Owning unexamined beliefs and values that separate and divide
5. Denying evidence of truth being distorted
6. Yielding to unresponsive and disappointing conversations
7. Lack of willingness to forgiveness and let go, releasing old hurts

As I talked with people and their stories unfolded, the inhibitors described below seem to be the behaviors they experienced in themselves or others most often. These inhibitors lay witness to their conversations as uninvited guests whose presence was felt, acknowledged or unacknowledged. It is when they went unacknowledged that the outcomes were less than satisfactory. As you read them, see if any are familiar to you and your preferred ways to respond. If you feel some discomfort, pay attention, it may be a signal that you might want to give it more thought.

Inhibitor #1: Tendency to Avoid confrontation♥

Most of us avoid confrontation at all costs This condition creates a severe silent divide between you and others. It thrives on the notion that if I confront you, I will lose you, you won't like me anymore, I won't belong to the group anymore, I'll be an outsider. Often there are political and social ramifications where you must determine if the cost is too high. So, you make a choice to avoid, at all possible cost, any confrontation that might "spoil things" as we know them. To speak up without worrying about the consequences requires great personal courage, and it is the path to freedom. Avoidance of confrontation is an example of living with a rigid and false security that causes erosion of spirit. You avoid having the real conversation externally, and the voices of rage carry on internally, repeating themselves over and over, giving you no relief.

The longer you remain silent, your emotional discomfort builds on itself. Thankfully, relief comes when you have finally had enough. When it becomes so unbearable, you either explode, retreat, or decide to give it a voice. Realizing there is another choice—a choice of developing what I call *confrontation with compassion,* where you speak from a caring and loving place that takes care of your soul. Your mind can be your best friend or your enemy. You can open, close, lose or change your mind at any moment. Have you ever found yourself thinking but not acting on this statement? *I was going to give them a piece of my mind.* That was the voice inside you wanting the real you to show up. But you did not show up...that piece of mind you wanted to give stayed inside you are hiding out. You and others can be transformed by sharing your mind. Mental noise is an internal distraction, it takes courage to expose who you are. After you have done all you know how to do, just be present...it is an opportunity to meet yourself face to face. To speak the truth as you know it to be.

TRUTH STORY:
Avoidance to Speaking what is on your heart

A very dear friend related her own truth story where she held on to a discomfort so long, that it made her heart ache. When she described to me the relief that came from having the courage to speak what was on her heart, she found herself wondering why it took her so long. Had she not faced her fears of possible loss, leaving unfinished business unresolved, she would have put her valued relationship in serious jeopardy.

Having had no children of her own, a young woman came into her life who became her daughter. She treasured the relationship with the new-found daughter. In her delight state, she called every day, for fear of losing contact. Over time, she began to feel a slight discomfort and noticed reluctantly that her daughter was avoiding her. Phone calls did not seem to be as welcomed as they were in the beginning. My friend had a constant internal struggle with herself for days, imagining the worse. She finally gathered the courage to have a conversation with her daughter about how she was feeling. Her daughter, in return, shared her own discomfort expressing relief to have the conversation. She, too, was feeling the pressure from so many calls, given her work and life demands it felt overbearing. She did not want to hurt her newly found mother's feelings and was not sure how to bring it up. She too had remained silent.

Both were having the same feelings and emotions and having not voiced them, they could not imagine that they were feeling and thinking the same things. After their talk, where they shared openly what was in their hearts, their relationship became more loving and stronger than it has ever been. What they both feared most was hurting one another's feelings, risking rejection, or abandonment of a relationship they valued.

They have now resumed a beautiful, healthy relationship where they know they can speak truthfully about issues that weigh on their heart. My friend related how at an early age, she learned from her parents that you did not talk about personal feelings or family issues outside the family. Family issues were considered a private matter and never should be discussed.

Once my friend found the courage to acknowledge her innermost feelings about her fears of possible: rejection, embarrassment, being dismissed, misunderstood, or a loss of a relationship and love. she was able to move through her fears finding relief in being her authentic self. There is a Native American saying that states, *"fear is what You grapple with until you find your courage."*

Remember, courage in the French translation means heart defined as your innermost feelings. Embrace and understand your motives so you will generate positive energy as you share your innermost feelings, no matter how your message is received. My friend clearly felt that the walls of separation came down when they both had the courage to share their innermost feelings.

What I have come to know is that when the intent is to live in compassionate light and loving spaces, the message will be received well. In our world where turmoil, untruths, and hurt seem to rule the day, it is important that your words are intended to heal.

REFLECTION 1.
BE STILL...ASK.... LISTEN....BE STILL

Reflection and Curiosity...What do you do to avoid confrontation? ♥

1. What are you doing or saying that does not allow your voice to speak your truth?

2. Why are you unwilling to confront what you feel is not true?

3. How does your fear of avoidance and confrontation influence what can happen?

4. Is your intent to feel empathy, compassion, and to create understanding?

5. What do you need to say or do differently to be at peace with letting go if you do not confront what violates you?

6. How do you want to show up differently?

REFLECTION 2.
JOURNALING....BE STILL...LISTEN...WRITE...BE STIL, READ

Inhibitor #2: -- Self-Justification the need to be right: ♥

Self-Justification is the position that hardens your view and closes you off to being open to another's perspective. It is often clouded by your personal truth and belief that what you believe is "RIGHT". It causes you to justify your position at all costs. The strategy most often used is to make the other person feel defensive or wrong and to hear what you want to hear rather than the truth of what has been said.

Many times, your beliefs are based on ideas you have not examined or self-deception that has no basis for truth, except what you have created in your head. You deliberately cultivate and look for evidence that justifies and supports your position of "rightness." You live in the space of denial of what truth is. This results in frustration from the other who is trying to get through to you. This makes you more rigid and less likely to consider another point of view. This position shuts you and the other person down to any possibility of dialogue where learning and personal growth can occur. It closes the door for opening a path for reconsideration or new possibilities for the relationship. Most times, all parties involved experience judgment or being judged. The result being mistrust and disappointment, leaving an imprint of genuine and deep hurt. How you respond to others is tied directly to your belief and values.

TRUTH STORY:
Rigid Self-justification leaves no room for empathy

This story occurred on my way back to the car repair shop. The driver picked me up at home. On the way we stopped at a stoplight and there was an abandoned sign that said "homeless, need to get back to Oregon." There was no person around. He said with distain in his voice, "I guess he got the money." He then went on to describe how homeless people were everywhere in the neighborhood. The police, according to him, came with dumpsters one day and threw all the shopping carts, where the homeless kept their stuff, into the dumpster. If they could not carry It, into the dumpster it went. Clearly, he thought this was fine. I did not.

I could not believe what I was hearing. In my mind, it was all that they had, and to just take away "their stuff" was to me inhumane. He went on to say that it cleaned up the street. I asked, what happened to the people? He said they moved to someplace else. Knowing he and I saw this situation very differently, I said, "I can't imagine what it would be like to be homeless and have the only things I owned, to keep my belongings in taken away like that." He just looked at me with a scowl on his face. There was dead silence. I only hope the silence meant he was at least giving my view some thought. He clearly believed he was right in his judgment of them and what happened to them. I certainly was thinking about his view for many days to come. Where was the empathy? It left my heart feeling so sad.

I thought back to a moment I had with my grandson years earlier when I was working with a homeless shelter in Boston. It was a bitter cold day and I had to deliver a report to the CEO from the work I had done with her and her staff. I took my grandson with me. As we entered there were men all over, some mumbling to themselves, some smelly; they were sitting or lying wherever there was space. My grandson took my hand and squeezed it. It was clear he was bothered by what he saw. He asked me why were these men here? I thoughtfully reflected and said some had lost their jobs, some were sick and had no place else to go, no home to go home to. He looked at me with tears in his young eyes and said, "nana, this is not right". This interaction caused me to wonder, when and why do we lose our voice and our sense of empathy for those less fortunate?

REFLECTION 1.
BE STILL...ASK.... LISTEN...BE STILL L

Reflections and Curiosity: What is your Justification for your need to be right? ♥

1. What causes you to need to be, right?
2. Can you think of a time when you needed to consider another point of view and did not?
3. Have you ever created false evidence to support your point of view?
4. Can you think of a time when you closed off new information and possibilities?
5. Can you remember when you had the opportunity to show compassion and empathy and blew it?
6. What do you wish you had done differently?
7. What values and beliefs do you hold that get in your way?

REFLECTION 2.
JOURNALING....BE STILL...LISTEN.... WRITE...BE STILL, READ

Inhibitor #3: Fear of Consequences: Standing in your truth alone ♥

It takes a lot of courage to be who you really are, when the world is asking you to be someone else. We spend our lives compromising to meet someone else's standard or view of who we should be. This requires us to hide out in a space we create in our own private world. We spend a lot of time on the pretend stage just trying to belong.

I encourage you to take a bow and move on and create your own script with you as the star, the producer, the writer, the actress/actor. Title this as **who I am**. Fear of being alone, not belonging, retaliation, and rejection provides actors that support the false image we present to the world. We dare not change the script or step out of line to be a person of our own choosing. To become an independent thinker and speak his/her truth is almost unimaginable — whether it's unacknowledged family issues, relationship tensions, work challenges, political affiliations, racial affiliations or religious beliefs or values that differ from the majority or minority.

There is evidence that when you are different or see things differently you find yourself standing alone. It seems everyone lines up behind the person who is leading the charge to demonize you. Most times it is out of their own fear that if they do not go along, they will be next. Facts get distorted, and the courageous truth-teller becomes demonized. Too

54

often, self-doubt appears in the psyche of the person who is telling the truth. It is a tough place to be because you seem to be in it all alone. As the person speaking the truth, you begin to wonder if it is all worth it.

I encourage you to stay your course: stand up and speak your truth. As you make your way through it, you may endure scars and wounds. Remember, this is your moment to be who you really are. Try it on. See how it feels. Quiet yourself and claim strength and power from your source from within. Embrace full responsibility to connect with what it is for you to do in this world. The good news is the wounds you sustained on your authentic journey will heal. You will discover the miracle and power of your own voice. This is your special moment to engage with yourself in ways you did not think were possible. Being venerable so you can see and feel it will be your gift to yourself. Your internal healing begins as a new life force appears – affirming your belongingness in the world.

The growth moments occur for you when you consider your values and as you listen and understand the values which others hold in their hearts and Why? This inward, outward look gives you the chance to make choices, adjustments, and friendly amendments to your courageous voice of truth. This moment is your moment. It is a way to acknowledge that you are growing, changing, and becoming the person you intend to be. It offers you the chance to show the world who you are.

Nikki Giovanni has a beautiful poem, stating, *"If I can't see out you can't see in either. How can you get to the truth if you won't allow looking in and seeing out?"*

The questions at the end of this chapter are designed to support you in your inquiry of yourself, looking in while, having the empathy and compassion to look outside yourself.

TRUTH STORY:
Taking Risk, what are you willing to lose?

This is one of our most feared possibilities not knowing what the consequences will be. None of us wants to be rejected, excluded, or lose those things that are dear to us and that we have fought so hard to attain and retain. To be rejected and/or excluded from family, friends, and work is an emotional drain on your energy and spirit. It hurts deep in your hearts and soul. Here is a powerful but sad story that illustrates the power of rejection when the possibility of not belonging and losing family influenced the choice.

After giving the keynote presentation at a women's conference, a woman came up to me and asked me my political affiliation. When I told her, she had a big sigh of relief. She then told me her story of how she lived a life where she had to pretend a political affiliation, she did not believe in. Her husband held beliefs different than her own; he had never taken the time to understand hers. He would have been appalled if he knew, and she was convinced he would leave her. He was teaching her sons what she considered hateful things. Yet, she did not have the courage to stand up to him, because she feared she would lose everything, her home, her children, and her financial well- being. She went on to say that If her friends discovered her actual affiliation, she would be alienated and considered a traitor. She and I met many times for coffee after that day and became friends. My heart wept for her; she saw no way out for herself. I provided emotional relief in the only place she felt safe, where she could speak what was true for her without judgment. Fear had overwhelmed her, and she exhausted herself with sadness. At some point, we have all lived in this space where we have silenced our own voice because of the fear of losing everything we love.

Freedom comes when we move through fear and free our own voice no matter what the consequence. Only you can decide if it is worth it to voice what is real and authentic for you. It is a choice of what kind of life you want to live.

REFLECTION 1.
BE STILL...ASK...LISTEN...BE STILL

REFLECTION and CURIOSITY: how does fear and taking risk inhibit you? ♥

1. What do you say or do when people of your own race or identity group say racist or disparaging remarks you disagree with?
2. What Is the personal risk you take for speaking up?
3. What is the risk for others?
4. What will you lose?
5. What will you gain?
6. Why does it matter if you are rejected by your group?
7. What can you do or say to inspire truth and healing?

REFLECTION 2.
JOURNALING... BE STILL...LISTEN.... WRITE...BE STILL, READ

Inhibitor # 4 – Owning Unexamined beliefs: Do you dare peek?♥

You hold dearly to beliefs that have served you, examined or unexamined. We look for others of like minds to reinforce our beliefs hateful or loving, true or false. Our beliefs stay in place, serving a purpose, affirming you are ok, and you tend to reject those who do not agree with your perspectives. This state produces personal dysfunctional behavior when beliefs and values are suppressed to please others.

You live in a world of self-generating beliefs, which remain primarily unexamined or tested. You cannot live your life without adding meaning or drawing conclusions based on your experience of the life you are living day-to-day. It is your experience of people, places, feelings, thoughts, or circumstances that determine how you react. This is what defines who you are. Our ability to be open to expanding our views and beliefs beyond what we are familiar with requires a personal commitment to become more aware of our own thinking and reasoning and making it visible to others. That is the "looking in" part. Then it is necessary to take the next step which is to look outside of yourself and to be genuinely curious as you inquire into what others are thinking. There is a Toni Morrison quote that states it this way, *"What's the world for if you can't make it up the way you want it?*

Unexamined Beliefs and Prejudice that belong to you

Living with unexamined beliefs that were taught to you at a young age is not uncommon. You understood intuitively that if what you spoke was not courteous or politically correct, that it was expected of you to not speak it out loud. This was accepted as normal behavior even when the truth was obvious. Beliefs simply stated are what you believe to be right or wrong, just, or unjust, this is what governs what you think, feel, do, or not do, say or not say.

Even today, if there is a belief that it will cause embarrassment or discomfort, it has become acceptable not to say anything. Political correctness has become misused serving a dual purpose, with outcomes that were devise, as well as, positive. One, it has pushed real conversations underground. Sometimes creating a narrative labeling people as being insensitive or not inclusive. This has caused defensiveness and uncomfortable relationship. This is ok, but it should not be left to exclude rather than explore increasing understanding to bring people together. Two, it has served a positive purpose to have people become more sensitive to others.

The conceptual belief that governs this practice has had intended and unintended consequences. It serves to remind you that unexamined beliefs do not serve us well, and sometimes they get in your way, leaving residue and scar tissue over many generations. When personal feelings are not voiced and are violated overtime, you become a prisoner to your feelings. You begin to experience your life force and spirit bereft of energy for living a joyful life.

What is going on internally is not visible to others. These emotional scars are internal; but make no mistake, they are real. They are buried just below the surface waiting for your permission to have a voice. Each of us knows what we feel inside, even when we have not given voice to it. Yet, intuitively, people who care for you know instinctively something is just not right. They may not be able to name emotional scars, but not naming them, does not mean they are not there. Clues are all around that go unnoticed or ignored.

Like physical scars, emotional scars are equally painful and reside in places where they cannot be seen. They lay dormant, occasionally, making their presence known, but unannounced, causing you to wonder. Where did that come from? When you hold on to unexamined beliefs that have been chosen for you, they can cause real internal conflict. Competing beliefs - old and new ones cause You to search for answers. As you question yourself, *"what do I really believe"?* You come to understand that conflicting beliefs, if suppressed, cause confusion, pain, and disappointment. It seems there is no place where your voice can be heard sorting it out, except in your head. This creates emotional noise that will not be quieted, it can only be dealt with by examining what you believe and why you believe it. These moments insist on clarity where change becomes an option, where you can make a different choice.

Dare to care enough to look within yourself with compassion and care to honor your experience. Dare to look for the internal signals that suggest you consider some necessary changes in yourself. Listed below are some clues to consider.

- Your humanity and aspiration are challenged and have grown weary and tired.

- You have a numbness of spirit and sad feelings prevails going unacknowledged.

- Your relationships are dysfunctional, and they are not authentic.

- Your Individual Spirit is deplete of energy.

- Laughter and joy are missing in your life.

- Unexpressed beliefs and values hold your truth hostage.

- Mental noise and chatter of internal voices are on-going distractors.

TRUTH STORY:
Beliefs unexamined with no room for change!

On a trip to Africa to facilitate a group of religious leaders who represented varied denominations of religious practices - Muslims, Pentecostal, Protestant, Anglican, and Catholic - I witnessed and became a target for a real stern lesson in rigid beliefs.

I was traveling with a black angel doll my daughter had made for me, in her words, "to watch over me and keep me safe." I took out the doll with a great deal of pride and shared it at the meeting with my religious group. An African-Anglican Priest was offended by my black angel doll. He looked at me with an intensity hardened by his beliefs and said," There are no black angels, only white ones." I thought he was joking, but the look on his face and tone of his voice made it clear to me he was not.

He held the belief that there were only white angels in heaven. No one in the group of ten said a word. There was an uncomfortable silence. I was shocked and baffled. It was clear that there was no way he could be convinced otherwise. His belief left no room for other possibilities. Rather than trying to convince him. I let it go and simply said. "For me, there are Black angels."

Sometimes, you must let it go and find a way to still be true to yourself. I will tell you this exchange changed our relationship. While I honored his belief, it was clear to me he could not honor mine. I reminded myself that preparing for new emotional growth sometimes requires withdrawal and stillness, allowing time for adjustment for where new thoughts and feelings can be considered.

TRUTH STORY:
Personal beliefs and snap Judgements

I was on a plane delighted at being upgraded to first class. I thought I could get some rest having just facilitated a very tough group of clients. I had a window seat and was getting settled in. My seatmate arrived, a young man who I looked at and then quickly dismissed, looking away. In my mind, I instantly dubbed him as a punk rocker; leather jacket, pink hair, ring in his nose. I thought to myself," oh great, we have nothing in common." I settled in my seat; eyes closed determined not to engage. After the plane got up in the air, he asked me if I minded having a political conversation. This seemed an odd question to me. My interest was perked up, and I said yes.

As it turned out, it was a conversation about racism and politics. It turns out it was more a conversation about standing alone and the loneliness he felt as a result. Once I agreed to engage, he then proceeded to tell me that he was in college and that all his college buddies had voted for a candidate he could not support. He voted for Obama. He assured me that if anyone knew he had, he would be ostracized and rejected by all his buddies, as well as his family. He felt hurt and was in genuine turmoil; he was lonely and could not resolve for himself what he could do about it. He knew he was not being true to himself by remaining silent. He simply was not willing to risk being an outsider. He talked about how painful it was at times. He shared how he hated himself for not saying what he really felt. As our conversation continued, I left room for him to trust me and speak his painful truth. We ended up having a deep heart-wrenching conversation, with both of us laughing and shedding some tears. I found myself fully engaged with him and liked him very much. We were as different as two people could be, yet we found common ground, simply by getting to know each other.

Later, when I was alone, I realized how I had stereotyped him. I had made up my mind about him in an instant and moved to judgment, based on my belief and preconceived notion of what a "white Punk Rock kid was. My instant conclusion had been that he had nothing in common with me, nor I with him.

Shame on me, how he was dressed had turned me off. I reluctantly chose to engage with him; and to my surprise, I found him delightfully funny and insightful. If I am honest with myself, I realize I would not have engaged with him on my own. It would have been a missed opportunity. I like to pride myself on my opinion of me as not rushing to judgment and giving people a chance to show who they are. I believe and accept the premise that when I sit in judgment, there can be no room for joy or love and certainly no room for conversations that matter. I was surprised and disappointed in myself as I noticed how easily I slipped into stereotyping this young man. My lesson here is I still have work to do. I am thankful I get another chance. Someone once said," you cannot hate someone up close; it is only when you keep them at a distance that hate can live."

It is only through compassion, positive energy, and acceptance of myself that I can forgive and dissolve the effects of my judgments. Thanks to this wonderful delightful punk rocker,

I relearned this valuable lesson which reminded me that when I allow space for precious differences without insisting on conformity or superiority, it is possible to listen to a painful story of a stranger and be open to forming unlikely relationships. We spoke openly to one another and made a heart connection that went far beyond the plane ride as seatmates thrown together by chance. We have talked several times since, and he has made determined steps forward towards living his truth.

TRUTH STORY:
I do not know you. An opening for prejudice, racial hatred

During the busing era in Boston, racial hatred was out of control. Adults and children from poor families in the Irish community were acting out based on fear, racial prejudice, and lack of experience and truthful exposure to black people. What they did not realize is that we as black parents were poor too. We just wanted a good education for our children just like they did. We wanted the same things, yet they saw us as the enemy. They saw us as a threat simply because they did not know us or have experience of us as neighbors. As Blacks we were different, "the other" who did not live in their neighborhood.

Rocks were thrown through school bus windows. A young boy was shot at from a rooftop into a football game in which my son was playing and my daughter was in the bleachers watching this horror. The young boy who was shot was paralyzed for the rest of his life. He is now dead.

There were many other incidents that are shameful and almost unimaginable. How could adults act this way? How could they teach their young children to throw rocks and shout racial slurs at people they did not know and had done them no harm? In my effort to understand, I took part in a conversation with a mother on the "other side," I chose to try to understand how she could engage in some of these hurtful actions. I asked her, "Why are you doing these hateful things, and teaching your children to hate? I have done nothing to you, nor have my children." She looked in my eyes and said with a tired, weary voice, "I don't know you or your children. We do not have Blacks living in our neighborhoods. We have nothing, we are poor, and if you take what little we have, then there will be even less for us."

I asked her, "do you really believe there is not enough for all of us?" She said, "No, I am just trying to survive." This gave me a window into her world that I was not aware of. She did not know my children, which left her room to create an image of us that was not real; we had become less than human to her, taking what little she had. That was the myth she held about us. I felt empathy for her, although I could not excuse her behavior or the behavior of her community. She told me that even though she did not agree with some of what was going on, her community felt strongly about preserving what they perceived as "their" right. If she did not fall in line, her children would suffer and be hurt and ostracized by her neighbors. She was not willing to risk standing up against her neighbors and community to use her voice to right a wrong.

We continued our conversation and were on speaking terms. I am not sure I influenced her thinking... maybe I did.... I hope so. It was a beginning, an opening for both of us. We were both challenged to look within ourselves to try to understand what being poor, labeled, misunderstood, and suffering lack causes in all of us. Speaking truth about the effects of poverty and privilege and where they collide cause harm and danger to all of us.

This aspect of our society must have a voice. If we are ever going to bridge the racial divide that exists between us, these are serious conversations that must be had. It will require creating safe spaces where a great deal of courage can flourish. Where truthful dialogue demands what could and should be done to heal deep wounds. Ta-Nehisi Coates said, and I quote: "We do not want facts to violate the myths: We do not want to let go of the way our experiences have organized things in our minds."

REFLECTION 1.
BE STILL...ASK...LISTEN ...BE STILL

REFLECTION and CURIOSITY: *What are the Beliefs that you own as your truths?* ♥

1. What are the beliefs you own and live up to that serve you? (list 5 of them)

2. What are the beliefs you hold that harm you and others?

3. What is the damage done to you or those you care about as you suppress your beliefs?

4. What is the emotional toll you are subjecting yourself to by not speaking up?

5. What is the best that can happen if you step forward to speak your true beliefs?

6. What if you are rejected? Is it worth the risk you are taking?

7. What do you need to do to feel safe, protected, and not alone as you state and act on your beliefs publicly?

REFLECTION 2.
JOURNALING...BE STILL...LISTEN...WRITE...BE STILL, READ

Inhibitor #5: Denying evidence of truth being distorted or denied ♥

Frequently, made-up facts are used to lie, distort, and squash the truth. This is a place where the truth is evident to everyone. Yet, no one has the courage needed to act or speak up to confront the lies evident to all. The consequence is individual and or group collusion where values and beliefs of individuals do not have a voice. Group think takes over drowning out truth for individual members. Cultural apathy becomes invasive, creating a cultural environment of uncomfortableness and untruths that goes unacknowledged.

An Emotional condition lives and breathes inside you that sanctions silence over truth. What has taken hold is not spoken about out loud to those who need to hear it. Secret conversation happens where only those who think like you can hear the truth of what you feel. You accept a firm belief that nothing you do will make a difference. Evidence suggests that those who hold this belief feel sincerely that there is too much to lose. You tell yourself, *I have seen this before; it will change for a minute, and eventually, things will go back to normal. So why bother?* You tell yourself that it is not worth the risk of being an outsider. What becomes accepted as normal, is simply an untruth that no one is willing to give a voice to. It is the poison pill of families, relationships, friends, political parties, and organizations.

Collusion and complicity to remain silent confirm untruths to be real when it is not so. Your complicit agreement by your silence over time destroys your integrity and the spirit of those around you.

REFLECTION 1.
ASK THE QUESTIONS, BE STILL...ASK...LISTEN...BE STILL

Reflection and Curiosity: Are you courageous enough to stand alone when the truth is being denied or squashed? ♥

1. How can you prepare yourself for possible rejection, standing up for truth to be told?

2. When have you witnessed or been complicit in distorting truth by your silence?

3. Who can you go to for support?

4. What do you need to do to find a place of silence to connect with your soul?

5. Have there been moments when you must stand alone to defend truth being told?

6. How did it feel?

7. What would you do differently next time?

REFLECTION 2.
JOURNALING BE STILL...LISTEN.... WRITE....BE STILL, READ

Inhibitor #6: Yielding to Unresponsive and Disappointing conversations ♥

Having unresponsive and disappointing conversations is one of the most frustrating human interactions most of you speak of. Often, you are invested in the person, vision, the work, or relationship. You want desperately to make it work. Yet, in its current form, it is just not working for you. Trying to have a conversation to make things better repeatedly goes nowhere and you feel ignored. Your opinions seem to not matter. You might be listened to, but you know intuitively that you have not been heard.

This is confirmed as evidenced by the fact that nothing changes in the circumstances, behavior, or the relationship. Most often, there is a strong denial from the other person that anything is wrong. They spend time being defensive or by justifying the behavior or actions they have taken. You experience their voice as constantly denying your feelings and perspectives, making you wrong. You decide it is just not worth the personal investment to keep trying. It feels sad and you are discouraged. It seems your best efforts are going nowhere. Disappointing conversations repeatedly cause your energy to become drained, and you feel exhausted. Eventually, you are faced with the realities of simply living with it, or letting it go.

The letting go part is never easy because it feels like you have failed yourself and the other person involved. If your choice is to give up, in doing so you carry with you the internal wounds of a voice unheard, a sadness for yourself. If you stay in and remain silent, you compromise your emotional wellbeing for the sake of keeping the peace as your voice remains dormant. It is important to understand and accept that the only person you can change is yourself. That realization can bring you peace of mind.

TRUTH STORY:
Conversations that expose truths

This is a story that all families experience at some point and may sound familiar to you. It is the story of secrets that everyone knows, yet no one speaks about in public. It is common to all of us. There are family secrets, that are no secrets at all, because everyone knows them. They just do not speak on it.

In this story, the daughter was a heavy drinker with erratic behavior, especially when drunk. Alcohol was disguised in fruit punch, no one was fooled about this deception. Family members tried politely to address the issue directly, and she was in adamant denial about the severity of the problem.

After several awkward attempts to talk with her to no avail, her vehement denial that she had a problem eventually won out.

Family members became tired of conversations going nowhere. Feeble efforts were made less frequently, and the continual denial broke hearts and silenced voices. The pretense that everything was ok lived with them all. They realized and accepted that there would be no response to their deep concern. They had to accept that until she was willing to acknowledge the problem and change her behavior, anything they might do would have no effect.

It has been years, and nothing has changed. No one speaks of it anymore to her, and rarely to each other. Yet, once in a while to one another, they lament how much it pains them to watch her self-destruct, and to see what it is doing to her physical and emotional wellbeing personally. They love her and hold out hope. Everyone is just emotionally tired, sad, and weary, living with deep regret. No one is willing to out her in public. It is only expressed in private individual conversations, so as not to embarrass her. The result is... nothing changes.

REFLECTION 1.
ASK THE QUESTIONS BE STILL...ASK...LISTEN...BE STILL

Reflection and Curiosity: How are you complicit in maintaining family secrets that are not true?♥

1. What do you and others need to say or do to change the family narrative?

2. What are your imagined inhibitors to speaking the unspeakable?

3. How do others see what you see, do they see it differently?

4. Have you colluded and become complicit by not exposing the truth?

5. How do you feel about the lack of responsiveness to your concern?

6. What action can you take to neutralize the situation?

7. What needs to happen or be said to contribute to emotional peace for all?

REFLECTION 2.
JOURNALING...BE STILL...LISTEN...WRITE...BE STILL, READ

Inhibitor #7: Lack of Willingness to Forgiveness and Let go, releasing old hurts: ♥

Forgiveness is a gift you give yourself and others. As an inhibitor, forgiveness is one of the most difficult things to do. If not done, it involves carrying around emotional baggage and holding on to deep hurts that keep old wounds open, which might otherwise heal. It is up to you to make peace with your inner-most feelings and move on. That does not mean keeping people or a person in your life that may be toxic for you. It does require looking beyond the behavior of the offender, perceived or real, and saying, "I forgive you."

It does not mean condoning an action or behavior. instead, forgiving provides you the opportunity to release negative thoughts and feelings and find the strength and courage to move forward. Old hurts and resentments are difficult to release. Until you do, it will stop you in your tracks and prevent forward movement in your life. It is possible that you will have to forgive yourself and the person or events more than once to completely release and let go of the hurts or harm that you feel inside you. You can do this!

TRUTH STORY:
Betrayal of a Friendship and valued relationship

Listening to this story brings back memories of places where relationships have caused me pain or hurt in my own life. It reminded me of where I got stuck on the wrong that was done to me. For a time, while the pain was fresh in my mind, forgiveness was out of the question. I finally moved on and let go, but it took time.

This story is about a 20-year friendship between two women. They traveled together, drank, and had fun together, went through family ups and downs together and finally in retirement moved to another state together. Their friendship was a sisterly bond which neither could ever imagine being broken. One was more financially stable and generously carried most of the cost for travel and entertainment and relocation. Judy who relied on her friend's generosity and benefited significantly, had no problem accepting being taken care of. After their retirement and moving to the new place, things begin to change. Judy begin to find fault with her friend. As they made new friends suddenly the relationship begins to change. Judy began to comment negatively about how her friend dressed or spoke and her friend was often criticized publicly, in an effort, to make her appear somehow less acceptable to others. She said "Judy appeared to be my friend, but her behavior puzzled and hurt me. It was as if she got satisfaction from making me look bad, tearing me down. She even went so far as to try to discredit me with my own daughter, speaking untruths about my behavior. This was when I had enough. I had to acknowledge and accept that our friendship was over." In her words, describing how painful it was, She stated "After all I did for Judy, how could she do this to me?"

The hurt and pain caused by this breech of friendship went so deep that when she spoke about what happened she said, "I hate her, and I will never forgive her." It is clear as she recounts the story that the hurt and pain still lives inside her. Until she can forgive herself, in her words for "being stupid, being used" and let go of the betrayal, she will not be able to let go of the past to move forward. She will not be free.

REFLECTION 1.
ASK THE QUESTIONS...BE STILL...ASK...LISTEN...BE STILL

***REFLECTION** and **CURIOSITY,** Who in your life in the past or present do you need to forgive?* ♥

1. What is keeping you from forgiving someone who has hurt you?

2. What do you need to do to forgive yourself?

3. How is the old baggage you are carrying holding you back?

4. What is the fear, hurt, or wound you will not let go of that keeps you from forgiving?

5. What do you need to do to begin to heal yourself?

6. What is the first step you will take toward forgiving? When?

7. What is the gift you give to yourself by letting go of the old script and writing a new one?

REFLECTION 2.
JOURNALING...BE STILL...LISTEN...WRITE...BE STILL, READ

FIVE
CREATING SUPPORTIVE
SAFE SPACE MATTERS

*What you do speaks so loudly that I cannot
hear what you say. - Ralph Waldo Emerson*

Accepting personal responsibility to act is your choice. Doing it in a safe and neutral place where there is comfort and security for all concerned enhances the possibility of an outcome that is supportive.

What is essential is to begin to explore what you can do to create a safer place for yourself and others to learn, listen, ask questions, and be asked questions to increase understanding. Everyone must feel protected with no worry about retribution for telling the truth to produce positive outcomes.

This raises the question about the safety and impact of e-mails, texting, twitter, Facebook, and other electronic methods for communicating to one another. Is this a safe place to have difficult conversations? Some would say yes, and some would say no.

In my opinion, far too many of us are afraid to have face-to-face confrontations and therefore we rely on electronic communication as a mask to hide behind. For many, the difficult conversation is perceived to be easier this way primarily because you do not have to face the person. Using electronic media while quick, convenient, and efficient, it diminishes our ability as people to have social face-to-face interaction with one another.

Fortunately, or unfortunately depending on your preference, using text messaging is now an accepted method of communicating. Things are said and documented and some of this is good. There is another aspect to it where bullying happens, harsh words are delivered leaving no way to see or feel the impact of your written words. It provides a false screen to hide behind, where words take on a life of their own. I believe the impact many times has unintended and intended consequences. It is no substitute for the real thing, you, and I in a room together, sharing who we are, what we think and feel. It makes us caring people. The jury is still out on the impact of this technology on person-to-person interaction.

Acknowledging the circumstances that support fear, which inhibits the "speaking up" voices to come forward gets in the way of feeling safe. Honoring individual experiences and memory of what has caused them to not feel supported requires a factual acknowledgement that radiates care, humility, and understanding. Your dialogue together must begin by having real talk, agreeing that a truthful conversation, no matter how difficult, is important to all parties. The following agreements must be discussed and agreed to:

- Examine and honor all experience, perspectives, and memory.
- Agree on what it takes to create an emotionally safe and supportive space.
- Acknowledge inhibitors big and small.
- Understand what you each want from the conversation.
- Ensure there will be no retribution or retaliation.
- Make sure that beliefs and values are understood, discussed, and not judged.

The conversations below are stories told with the intention to support reflection and contemplation, looking inward and outside yourself to embrace the point of view of others. It is more important to know what is going on inside you to allow yourself clarity on to see what is going on outside yourself. Be aware that each conversation can be tangled up with others as you unravel them. There will not be one version of the truth. All truths spoken must be examined with thoughtfulness and appreciation of the "other voice to establish feelings of trust. Beliefs might need to be stated and accepted several times before you can reach a place of feeling heard and safe. Understanding individual beliefs has real value when you understand what holds them in place. It is the stories behind them that help you with empathy and understanding illuminating a way forward.

TRUTH STORY:
Feeling safe and supported while speaking Truth

Having a safe place that is comforting and free from intimidation is essential. This means thinking through where there is a space that is neutral and provides comfort and security. It means more than just a space but a welcoming environment that is not distracting to either party while they are discussing their concerns and expressing their viewpoints.

In this story a young woman was being bullied by a schoolmate. She took a long time to speak up about it and when she did the school official in the principal's office did not take it seriously and nothing was done. They felt that she was overreacting. She did not feel safe at school and was frightened most of the time. When her parents finally became aware of the problem and intervened, they could not understand why she would not go to the principal's office to work things out. The young girl was embarrassed because she did not "stick up for herself". She had no faith in the school's ability to keep her safe and did not want to discuss it in the office where she was not believed or supported. Her complaints had been viewed as unwarranted, because the girl who was the perpetrator was popular and liked by her peers. Her parents were not satisfied with the administration's response and withdrew their daughter from the school. Her complaints were never addressed. Leaving seemed to be the only option. She was willing to speak up and was not supported when she did. This is not ok.

This 2nd story is about what happens when what you believe to be true and reality about your culture are at odds. Taking actions may cause you emotional discomfort and family disharmony that feels less than safe.

The mother in this story knew that for a Latino girl living stateside it was important that she get the best education possible. In her husband's view it was not important for a Latino girl to get an education. Her duty was to marry and make a good wife. Their beliefs were at odds with one another and it was clear in the culture that you did not go against your husband's wishes. This meant that as the mother she would have to make a difficult decision that would cause great disharmony in her home.

She did what she thought was right, defying her husband and her culture. She secretly enrolled her daughter in a program, portraying it as a temporary program. There was no support for her taking this stand, she had to be misleading to make it happen. She enrolled her daughter in a program that began her daughter's journey in education. Her bravery challenged every belief her culture had taught her. She realized that what she had been taught to believe was not what she believed to be true today specifically, for her daughter. She knew there could be serious consequences of emotional and physical safety. It could have cost her marriage, yet she persisted by supporting her daughter through high school, and college. She believed in her daughter and that translated to her daughter believing in herself. Her daughter is extremely successful today because old beliefs were tossed aside and replaced by the mother's courage to act on what she believed was best for her daughter.

REFLECTION 1.
BE STILL...LISTEN...BE STILL

Reflections and Curiosity: WHAT CAN YOU DO TO Feel safe looking outward and looking inward? ♥

1. What do you need to do to feel safe and supported taking an unpopular stand?
2. How can you help create a safe space for yourself and others, where truth can be spoken?
3. What fears do you have, what fears do others have?
4. Can you start by acknowledging your/others fears, values and beliefs?
5. How will you celebrate beginning courageous conversations?
6. What are your next steps to continue dialogue or to manage completion?
7. What cultural beliefs do you need adopt or let go of?

REFLECTION 2.
JOURNALING...BE STILL...LISTEN...WRITE...BE STILL, READ

SIX
COMMITMENT TO COURAGEOUS CONVERSATIONS

The questions which are asked of oneself begin, at last, to illuminate the world, and become one's key to the experience of others. - James Baldwin

To move forward and have these tough conversations requires personal courage, internal inquiry, and the determination to look beyond what you think is truth. There are helpful questions you can ask to understand and clarify your intentions as you prepare for your conversation. Your focus must be on generating positive energy, no matter how your message is received. The questions to explore are:

- *How can I keep myself open?*

- *How can I put aside anger, blame, attitude, or my need to be right, so I am heard?*

- *How can I prepare myself to listen and respond to what others must say?*

It may mean moving out of your comfort zone for what you and others perceive as the *"normal"* way for you to act. As Maya Angelou says, *"in this normal state, you will never meet the amazing you."*

Experience has revealed, when attitudes are in check, when intentions are clear, when words are intended to **heal and not hurt,** there is a better chance of being heard, a better chance to engage, a better chance to listen, and a better chance to ask questions. It is in this space, that you can begin to discover your amazing self and the amazing self in others.

- *For most of us. It's just too hard to confront the unknown, and it is scary because you do not know what is on the other side. Sometimes It seems safer to just say nothing in the moment. But there is something only you can do... Speak your truth to the person who most needs to hear it. Your voice is the bridge to the truth and the way forward. Your only path to inner peace and relief is giving yourself the courage to speak truth from your own heart, with your own voice. Your words are the voice of your soul, it is the bridge you walk across for internal peace.*

It is important to order your steps, remembering it starts with you. Acknowledge your fears as you open to new possibilities, with a renewed willingness to expand your viewpoints, to hear another person's voice, and consider perspectives different than your own. Remember, a courageous conversation takes a sincere personal commitment of time to invoke authentic expressions of your innermost emotions. It is your choice to make room for the emotions of others to visit with and have an honorable interface with your own.

One conversation is not enough to chart a new course that is based on mutuality, trust, forgiveness, and courage. Be committed to engaging until you feel your voice has had its say, and that the other person feels the same.

Why will you speak, and What will you say? It is serious business to decide to take the step to speak up and say what is the truth. The story that has been told is just not so. This is how I see it and experience it. This is where I stand. Speaking truth to power and to those we care for deeply is serious business. It offers you a chance to take risks that inspires others and opens the door for more questions than answers.

Truth-telling Commitment Steps: *Do it... start now!*♥

How do we begin to have the conversations that matter, the conversations that will make a difference in our lives? *Why haven't I done it? How do you do it?... What steps must you take? ... What choices do you want to make?*

A list of essential commitment steps is outlined for your consideration and action to support your commitment as you claim your voice. They must be taken in sequence to be most useful to get powerful relational outcomes. Once the conversations begin, do not be surprised at what you may discover. Prepare yourself to be amazed at what will surface once you fertilize the grounds for dialogue and truth. Once the conversation begins, it is destined to be an "aha" experience for everyone who has an open mind, open heart, and open ears...

Self-Reflection: Looking in and looking out: An unexamined life is a life worth not living.

You have heard the phrase "Where are you coming from?" You need to know what that place is. This requires self-reflection, which does not mean becoming so absorbed with self that nothing else matters. Self-reflection is a gift you give yourself by gently looking inward. This inward look is to reacquaint yourself with the values and beliefs you hold that provide guidance to your behavior and words used in your external world. It also requires you to honor what is going on outside yourself. There is a world out there that belongs to others and a world inside you that belongs to you. These place holders are where values and beliefs represent yours and other perspectives for you to consider repeatedly. Intention must be acknowledged and understood. Again, *why will you speak?* and *What will you say?* It is serious business to take the steps to speak up and say, *this is my truth.* Here is where the work begins, with you.

Questions for Self-reflections: Looking in with curiosity - looking outward seeking wisdom and surprise and understanding♥

1. How can you position conversations so you are heard and so you can listen?

2. How can you honor what is inside you and honor your external reality?

3. What can you do to understand your values and beliefs, as well as those of others?

4. What is the benefit for you to release shame, blame, and judgment and adjust beliefs?

5. What do you need to do to make a place for truth with compassion, empathy, and understanding for yourself and others?

- **Allowing the clouds to part to make way for the sun:**

It takes a personal commitment from you and the person you value enough to have the conversation with. Remember, in the story shared earlier what you believe colors your world like the clouds. It is an inside job, looking in with curiosity. It is an outside job, requiring wisdom and surprise. It is time to begin an inquiry from within to prepare you to look outside yourself and expand your world view. It is a little bit like the weather reports to prepare you for what is to come. High pressure and low pressure determine the conditions.

Let us get ready to inquire within.

- **Can You Name and claim** the fear and beliefs you hold, acknowledge them, and step forward courageously? Releasing all the old stories you have come to believe.

- **Will you Free your voice** inside your head to speak what is on your heart, and affirm the real authentic you?

- **Can you embrace the opportunity** to take care of unfinished business before it is too late? Relax in your imagination and create your new truth story, imagine what you want.

- **Will you commit to understand and listen to others with your heart open even when their ideas, words, and behaviors conflict, with your own?**

- **Can you rejoice in your choice to do it differently because you choose to?**

- **Are you willing to discover the person** inside you who is fantastic and has always had a voice that matters? It is your voice that has been waiting to be set free.

- **Are you willing to** rewrite the script that honors you and others who are a part of your life journey?

Truth-telling commitment pathway... ♥

Step 1. Get clear with yourself about your intentions.

Step 2: Ask the person if they are willing and open to having a conversation?

Step 3: Choose a neutral and safe place to talk with one another, and a time that works for both.

Step 4: Accept and agree on a truthful agenda and agree to speak, hear, listen, and ask questions for understanding.

Step 5: Believe and accept this as a lesson in humility, a growth opportunity for everyone involved.

Step 6: Ask yourself, "What can I change in myself to make things better and bring healing to the situation?"

Step 7. Be willing to make a change based on what you have learned. Remember, what we think we know does not leave space for what we do not know.

Step 8: Be patient. Allow space for reflection. Take a step forward to continue, start again, or let go.

Let us continue...

Conversation I: ♥

RELEASE: The old values and beliefs stories. Listen, ask questions, and welcome questions. Acknowledge and make visible what the new story is. Agree on what the new truth is and make the commitment to move forward together.

You must begin the process by making a firm commitment to the relationship, or from the leader if it is an organization, to acknowledge what it is, and to stay firmly committed to the work, giving time and resources (human and financial) to the Courageous Conversations work.

Courageous conversations do not just happen: You must create a safe space where voices feel free to be heard without judgment. It is a slow process because trust must be established and reinforced with visible, consistent behaviors that support a new way of being together. There must be a serious commitment to the investment of time and dollars that demonstrates that this work is important.

Conversation 2: ♥

RELAX: Honor the person's individual memory and disappointments.

This step is often missed because it takes time and a sincere desire to understand without standing in judgment. Everyone carries a history of their experiences, aspirations, desires, dreams, disappointments and wounds from words unspoken or words not heard. This must be facilitated with compassion and the intent to honor, listen carefully, ask questions, and be willing to answer them.

Conversation 3: ♥
REJOICE: in the possibilities of renewed relationships/ community that include collective voices.

Take seriously the voices of individuals telling their story that speaks of their history and honors their description of their reality and experience. Their spoken words inform the creation of what the possibilities are for a new story and a future together. Intentional, thoughtful, patient listening, and learning must be present to take in what is being said. Sustaining the momentum is essential to build belief in the possibility of ongoing courageous conversations. It cannot be a stop and go effort. Each person's voice and behavior must model and internalize the importance of the work. Everyone must be held accountable for its integrity. Leaders must be consistent, intentional, and steadfast. They must model with their response and behavior that it is safe to speak personal truths. Truth stories must become a value, providing time and space for ongoing discussion, frequently checking the pulse of how it is going or not going.

It is essential that feelings are honored, voices are heard, and the truth that is told is honest and made visible to the collective community more than once. Stories that capture the essence of what is occurring are essential as the relationships and community re-builds itself. Reinforcement of agreed-on new practices and behaviors must be held as sacred. This cannot be treated as a "nice to do when we get around to it." It is not the so-called "soft stuff."

Examining relationships and behaviors is hard to do. It requires a commitment and dedication to dialogue and time for reflection. This is not a comfortable journey; it is tough in the beginning. Once it becomes a part of your daily practice, it makes relationships and conversations so much easier.

Conversation 4:♥
REWRITE THE SCRIPT: Invest in creating a new story. Your story is like no other. It inspires an enduring personal or organizational LEGACY

That speaks to defining Who you are; What you are; What you dare to be: What you dare to dream together. You can inspire hope to support the foundation for truth to sustain itself. Legacy work builds on the dreams of individuals; it does not matter if it is your family, a relationship, or an organization or just yourself. It must come together as a collective dream which is articulated and aspired to by all.

The courageous conversations made visible bring a life force to individuals and organizations that set the foundation for investing themselves with the determination to create a Legacy of their own choosing.

SEVEN
TRUTH-TELLING
DAILY PRACTICES

*Simple truths reveal themselves when you ask the right
questions, listen for understanding and cultivate genuine
curiosity and caring. - Erline Belton*

You might be wondering by now, *when should you tell your
truth?* I have a simple guideline for truth-telling. *If
speaking what is on your heart is intended to heal, then speak
it, if it is meant to hurt, then keep your mouth shut.*

Young children's voices of innocence are a blessing and a
light that can show us the way in this crazy-wonderful world.
They mercifully have not learned political correctness or when it
is not proper to say certain things. They have not learned how to
pretend to just keep life comfortable, creating a false safe and
silent reality. It is a joy and sometimes hilariously funny and
embarrassing when a child gives voice to what we all know to be
true, but do not have the courage to speak out loud. No doubt, you

can remember a time when you had to suppress laughter or pretend not to know the truth when it comes out of the mouth of a child.

There are obvious examples of silent voices that exist in every family, in personal relationships, and in organizations, both public and private, where the truth goes unacknowledged. Where you have experienced an unexamined belief that says, "the truth is not welcome here so just shut up."

You could add dozens of scenarios witnessed in your life as your own true stories – stories where stress, strain, and blame define the daily interactions between people in your life. We see it sprinkled throughout our lives, in our households, at work, and relationships, distant and close. Why is this so? *Why do you allow and collude with withholding the truth, not speaking, what is the unspeakable? Why do you make a choice to live with the stress, tension, hurts, anger blame, shame, grief, and disappointments?*

What will it take for you to be the brave solo warrior called forth to have the courageous conversations—the conversations that everyone is desperate to have happen, yet no one is willing to be the first one to initiate them?

Truth-Telling daily practices... ♥

Do you have the will to support a daily practice of speaking what is true for you, modeling truth telling for those you care about who touch your life? Remember the stories of the children who speak their unfiltered raw truths that you admire. That sometimes causes us to laugh. Are you willing to go there? We do not often think about what we say to friends, colleagues, family, or our children until it happens. Then we are left with the question, "Why did I mention that?" or "Why didn't I say what I really feel?" Feelings of momentary regret, self-disappointment visit us in these moments of little white lies, which we think are OK, and the big lies which we know are not ok. In these awkward moments, we tell ourselves that "little white lies are ok...," but are they? Do they allow you to be fully who you are or are not? The daily truth practices below will begin to allow you to get closer and familiar with your authentic voice if you engage yourself in speaking truth to you. Remember, Saying yes to you means you are saying no to someone else, that is ok. You can get comfortable with saying no, it just takes practice. Can you take the time to be in a quiet space allowing a moment, for you to be in charge when the characters in your heads are reeking turmoil and confusion looking for answers? It is all up to you. Do you choose stillness, or will you continue to entertain the mental noise causing distractions, which supports indecision and confusion?

Practice daily truth, creating quiet moments; to become aware of where you are on the scale of 1-5; this is a personal acknowledgment and awareness of where you are, not a judgment. It allows you to rewrite the script as you like it.

Thoughts to consider ♥

- *Think of self-acknowledgment as a wise internal voice that offers up empathy and self-compassion.*

- *Let go of judgment as the harsh voice that insists on instilling guilt, criticism, and shame that seeks an audience.*

- *Be your own mirror and stay in your acknowledgment space, let it be your moment of accepting what is true for you, please.*

- *Know, it is only here in this space that you begin to understand how your values and beliefs are tied to how you respond.*

- *Let go of the current version of who you are and become the person you want to be.*

- *Laugh at yourself and have fun with it…. find self-love and recognize and embrace your authentic voice. As Michael Jackson sings: "I am looking at the man in the mirror, asking him to change his ways," no message could have been any clearer, if you want to make the world a better place take a look at yourself and make that change.*

Once you acknowledge where you are, it is time to get real about how you are showing up, telling your truth to yourself and others. I suggest journaling to track your behaviors so you can capture patterns and habits. Some of which you will want to keep and others you will want to let go of or change.

However, you choose to record yourself always start by jotting down the date, time, and place, noting where you are and how you are feeling, and the people involved. This becomes important when you are looking back at the circumstances and patterns that represent you to the world.

I wish you many moments of revelations with insights that cause you to shake your head in wonder, laughing, crying, smiling, and accepting what you said or did not say without harsh judgement. Be welcoming of yourself as you accept knowing the truth about you, in all your ways.

DAILY TRUTH PRACTICE — TRUTH Mirror Guide Scale ♥

1. I disappointed me.
2. I listened to increase my understanding, caring about the "other".
3. I need to get clear on my values and beliefs to know where I stand.
4. I am getting there I could have done better.
5. I know, and others know where I stand.
6. I let others know my true position.

Use the Truth Mirror Guide Scale to answer the following questions:

1. Do I let others know my true position? ____
2. Do I go along to get along? ____
3. Do I deny my truth for the benefit of others? ____
4. Do I withhold truth for fear of hurting feelings? ____
5. Do I shame myself by pretending certainty or expertise? ____
6. Do I silence my voice leaving things unsaid? ____
7. Do I take a stand when values or beliefs differed? ____
8. Did I say yes when I meant no? ____
9. Did I say no when I meant yes? ____
10. What were the moments when I felt fear? Why? ____
11. Did I stand alone accepting the consequences? ____
12. Did this encounter make me proud of who I am? ____

EIGHT
YOU CAN DO THIS;
SHOW UP AND SPEAK-UP

As You think, and act so shall you become.
- BUDDHA

♥ Are you willing to continue to live in the space of *"if only I had"* or *"I wish I had"*?

♥ Are you willing to uncover the voice that is anxious to be heard – a voice that can proudly say, "I said it"? Are you willing to let go of your position or perspective where blame and judgment live, to experience incredible freedom?

♥ Are you willing to forgive the bumps in relationship or circumstances to find a better way?

♥ Are you willing to support and encourage one another offering new ways of being and thinking together? Are you willing to care enough and to love?

I urge you to name and claim the fears that hold you back and acknowledge them, then let it rest, let it go. Free the voice inside your head to speak so it can affirm the real authentic you. Discover the person inside you who has always had a voice that matters, it has just been waiting to be free.

The early stage of engagement is about uncovering deeply held beliefs, with a sincere investment in engagement to rebuilding an individual's and community's trust. Sharing collective stories is a powerful force because we all have stories. The focus must be on engagement, dialogue and listening.

I strongly believe that an independent outside trusted voice, a coach that values relationship, and human rhythms and dynamics can be useful if you need a supportive voice to begin the journey with you. He or she must be independent, enter with compassion and humility with a clear intent to listen, learn and tell the truth story as it is. All voices, whether they are dissenting or supportive, deserve to be heard. The owners of the precious stories that are told must be engaged, their voices validated making visible the truth about who they are, what they believe and how they want to live and work together. This is a critical stage for all involved. The truth must be raw, honest, and recognizable, no matter who is implicated as good, bad, or indifferent. It is imperative that no judgment or blame exist.

To create the safe space we all need, *Courageous Conversations* must be spoken, earning trust continually by modeling behavior and building the belief that it's ok to speak what is true for you; that *Courageous Conversations* can be had, and nothing bad happens to you. When fear emerges, acknowledge it. Remember fear is there to protect you, but you must acknowledge its presents. It can be an inhibitor paralyzing you to inaction as well as, a cautionary when you are in danger. It can also be a stimulus and a motivative force when courage is required, allowing you to do things you never thought you could. If we have courage, then all our other qualities will slowly emerge. Courage is there waiting eagerly to stand with you, as you stand in your truth revealing who you are.

Honor and celebrate the authentic voice within you. Therein resides pearls of internal wisdom that lets you know when something is just not right, or when it is right. It is called intuition or a hunch. If you move into silence and listen to that voice and allow yourself to trust it, you will have the strength and courage to say what needs to be said. If you are thoughtful and reflective, claiming where you want to stand, your heart can be filled with compassion and forgiveness for yourselves and others.

It is a truth that you have, a unique view of the world you live in. That is why you are here in this space and time. The personal journey that matters is in finding your gift of voice that speaks from your heart. Speaking with your own voice frees you to be who you choose to be. This is the place where you will discover the very purpose you have been born to live, play in, and contribute to. No matter who you are, or what you do, your voice matters to the world.

I invite you to hold dear to this Virtue as you step into your journey: in stillness, the clouds will disappear when you are in touch with your sacred and precious self.

Oh, what a world we can create together **as you dare to embrace the beauty and truth of who you are when you stand up and show others who you are.** Your inspiration will flow freely to others as you live your life's purpose as you intend, full out with joy, compassion, truth, and love.

Enjoy your life journey adventure. Embrace curiosity, wonder, surprise and continuous learning. Allow the wisdom inside you to becomes your constant companion and guide. You have a delightful obligation to bring your highest and best self forward and to bring out the best in others. It is your personal responsibility to make the spot where you stand in our world beautiful.

YES, you can do this...... take that first step, **be on your way forward, show-up and speak-up. Embrace your internal and external voice. Always remember, this is the place where your inner-most feelings that lay on your heart reside. Where your beautiful, loving, courageous voice lies in waiting, patiently, FOR you to free your spirit and your soul as you, hear your own voice.**

You are amazing ♥

Blessed be you, always walking with a loving and truth spirit ♥

Erline

105

ABOUT THE AUTHOR

Ms. Belton has served on several corporate and non-profit boards of directors. She held a Teaching fellowship at Tufts University, her alma mater and other university appointments.

The Mission of The Lyceum Group is to influence societal and workplace thought leaders, to explore laser-focused conditions to support legacy creation through life coaching and healing truth telling conversations that exposes myths to organization and individuals. She believes that our world is changed and healed by the truth being told openly, as new safe spaces are prepared to explore myths and expose what is true as a path forward together.

She believes that value-based decisions produces world cultures that can nourish us all and honor our uniqueness. Her life's work is to be of service to others in their search for truth-based principles, values, and beliefs that support people and the work they do.

Prior to the creation of The Lyceum Group, Ms. Belton held several Executive level positions in Corporate America. Her current work extends beyond the United States to international markets. Ms. Belton has been engaged as a consultant, life coach, keynote speaker for leadership conferences and holds two exclusive workshops a year focused on Legacy creation and truth telling.

Erline is honored to be spoken of by clients as an organization healer, to her surprise. She feels passionate and honored to do her work as she practices her unique artform that focuses on creating loving and caring conditions for courageous truth telling and Legacy creation, engaging her heart and head in service to others.

Your Voice Matters: Courageous Conversations You Dare to Have is Erline Belton's second published book. Her first published book was A ***Journey That Matters: Your Personal Living Legacy.*** She resides in Marion/Roxbury Massachusetts and Phoenix, AZ.

READERS
GUIDE

This section is intended to allow you to reflect on what you have read and how to integrate its meaning into your everyday living. You may use it on your own or share it with other readers. As you tell your stories to one another be as truthful as you can. Allow emotions to be by your side, no matter if they are joyful or sad. It is important to let each person have their moment to share. The group role is to listen with their hearts open and to ask questions to increase understanding. I recommend you sit in a circle so you can see one another as you share what is on your hearts. What you share are your stories, and the gift you give is to share your experience of your living with others. May you learn and grow alone or together as you share your voices....

Remembering that your voice matters…enjoy. ♥

May you find and live your highest and best incredible life…from my heart to you with LOVE ♥ *Erline*

QUESTIONS FOR GROUP OR SOLO DISCUSSION

1. What story or questions in the book felt like they were speaking directly to you?

2. What is your earliest memory of speaking your truth? What was the consequence?

3. Describe a time when you were scared to speak up? What held you back?

4. What story in the book caused you to take a deeper look at yourself?

5. When was the first time you realized that people lie? How did you feel?

6. Do you have an inner-most truth that lays on your heart, that needs a voice?

7. Describe a time when you did not speak up and wished you had?

8. Describe a time when you were courageous, and your voice surprised even you?

9. Describe a myth in your life or work that you know has no truth, why does it continue?

10. When you took the daily Truth mirror guide, What did it tell you about yourself?

11. Who do you need to have a courageous conversation with? What is the topic?

12. What is the one injustice that you would not tolerate by being silent?

13. What 3 beliefs and values guide how you show-up and speak-up in the world?

14. What do you want to work on going forward so you show up as you please?

15. What support do you need? What will you do to get it?

16. What do you want to share with the author about what you have learned?

**Erline, welcomes your comments
and would love to hear your stories.
♥.... erlinebelton@gmail.com**

NOTES ♥

NOTES ♥

_____

_____

_____

_____

_____

_____

_____

_____

_____

_____

_____

_____

_____

_____

_____

_____

_____

_____

_____

NOTES ♥

_____
_____
_____
_____
_____
_____
_____
_____
_____
_____
_____
_____
_____
_____
_____
_____
_____
_____
_____

NOTES ♥

_____
_____
_____
_____
_____
_____
_____
_____
_____
_____
_____
_____
_____
_____
_____
_____
_____
_____
_____